I Can't Make Lunch Today.

I Can't Make Lunch Today.

Recollections and resources gathered from one family's cancer journey.

BRIAN, MADISON, AND BRAYDEN FOREMAN

ISBN: 1540463443
ISBN 13: 9781540463449
Library of Congress Control Number: 2016919350
CreateSpace Independent Publishing Platform
North Charleston, South Carolina

Gratitude

Throughout this book, I thank many people for their friendship and true acts of kindness.

A family's cancer journey can be one of loneliness. The disease can isolate patients and their caregivers, leaving them to ride out many storms in uncharted waters. Mercifully, we were not alone.

We gained our strength and the will to move forward from the goodness of family, old friends, specialists, community organizations, and many new folks we met along the way. You were our inspiration.

To the many doctors, nurses, technologists, administrators, and volunteers that understood our fight and eased our physical and emotional pain: We appreciate YOU for the time you took to listen, answer many questions, hold our hands, and offer shoulders on which to cry.

To my children, Madison and Brayden: you are my world. Your participation, patience, and understanding in the creation of this book have not gone unnoticed. You have gone through so much in your young lives and are remarkable individuals. No parent could be more proud. I am grateful for you both.

To my wife Marnie: soul mates from the first time we saw each other. You are amazing; the most incredible and dynamic person I have ever met. Thank you for our time together.

To Marie Beswick-Arthur: the world is a small place! I am so grateful that we met and collaborated on this project. You made the process seamless. Your professionalism was ever present in guiding us through a difficult time to create "our story".

Introduction

We're all in the arena: fans in the bleachers, and players on the bench with coaches flanking their teams. The referee and the linesmen are in place. A volunteer runs the clock while another records stats. In the stands, managers hand out newsletters, and a dedicated parent sells fifty-fifties; even the Zamboni driver and custodian have each bought one. Out in the lobby, more helpers run the concession. Game on.

A team player and devoted supporter of many, Marnie was never alone. Neither would she ever consider abandoning anyone in need.

As we prepared for New Year's, to welcome 2013, Marnie, (44), received 'OUR' diagnosis. Of course, the disease officially resided in her body, but affected, and therefore redefined, our family: husband, Brian (46) daughter, Madison (15) and son, Brayden (11). Her cancer changed our lives, that of our community, and introduced us to a whole new team.

Her cancer can change your life too. For in the great Canadian tradition of 'perseverance'—developed to plough through snowdrifts while walking against double digit wind chills (only to be fortified by concession coffee at chilly arenas)—we believe in teamwork.

**Marnie measured her performance by participation.
When, eventually, Marnie said, 'I can't make lunch today,'
we knew our journey had shifted to another level.**

We know that there will be days you or your loved ones can't make lunch either. While no two families' cancer journeys are alike—socioeconomics, geography, and personal dynamic are family specific—grief is a profound equalizer.

In fulfilling Marnie's legacy, we assure you that you are not alone. We intend everyone—patient, spouse, child, grandchild, parent, friend, caregiver, acquaintance, or a combination of the preceding list—receive support.

Weeks after Marnie's diagnosis, I sent out the first of many emails. As with a small act that is neither planned nor identified as a project, it took on a life of its own.

After Marnie's passing, the emails became this book, recounting our family's experience and informing on myriad topics. We continue to work tirelessly to fulfill the needs of those touched by cancer.

**We sincerely wish we did not have in common
that which we have in common
—that word 'diagnosis' and its hit-from-
behind, bullying cousin, 'Cancer'—
but until such time as this disease has retired,
we'll embrace Marnie's spirit (and that of many
others) as we 'Fight Like A Girl'.**

First Period

One

PLAY BY PLAY

January 3, 2013

TO: Friends and Family
FROM: The Foreman Family
SUBJECT: Marnie

Hello,

We hope that you have all had a great holiday season, and that you are off to a Happy and Healthy 2013.

We wanted to share some news that we received this week around Marnie's health. In December she discovered lumps under her armpit and on her breast.

She went in to see her GP right away and was then sent in for a biopsy. On Wednesday of this week, we received confirmation that she has been diagnosed with Ductal Carcinoma, and that it has spread to her lymph nodes. This is a very common type of breast cancer and is treatable.

After the initial shock, the anger, and the fear, Marnie is in a good place, and is ready to fight this awful disease. We have seen a surgeon, and are awaiting a confirmation date for her operation. This will be followed by chemotherapy and radiation.

You are our dear friends. We are asking for your prayers, love, and support as we go through this journey and kick cancer in the ass.

Together we will do this!

Brian, Marnie, Madison, and Brayden

January 9, 2013

TO: Friends and Family
FROM: The Foreman Family
SUBJECT: Update on Marnie

Hello,

Thanks to all of you for your replies to Marnie's news. We love all of the e-mails, texts, and phone calls. Your displays of support are really appreciated and help us get through the daily emotions.

We, as a family, have had a lot to digest and think about this past week about surgery and our options. We have consulted with many people in the health-care field as well as friends who have gone through this journey, and are confident that our decision is the best one that will kick this cancer in the ass!

We are very pleased with the medical team that she has been assigned by CancerCare as Dr. Ethel Macintosh and Dr. Ed Bushel are highly regarded in their respective fields.

Marnie is scheduled for surgery on Monday January 28th and will undergo a double mastectomy, as well as having several lymph nodes removed from her armpit. We are positive this is the best path to take as it significantly reduces our odds for Breast Cancer to come back. She will spend 3-4 days in the hospital and then come home to recover for 6-8 weeks.

We will continue to update you on her progress as she goes through her journey.

All our love,

Brian, Marnie, Madison, and Brayden

TIME OUT

*"If ever there is tomorrow when we're not together...
there is something you must always remember. You are
braver than you believe, stronger than you seem, and
smarter than you think. But the most important thing
is, even if we're apart... I'll always be with you."*

**CHRISTOPHER ROBIN (FROM WINNIE
THE POOH) — A.A. MILNE.**

RECAP

We were in shock, of course. Google any cancer website and you'll find a list of feelings associated with receiving the initial diagnosis: fear, anger, disbelief, guilt, loss of control, worry, hope. We each went through our individual versions, and, as a family, we moved swiftly from shock to schedule.

COACH'S CORNER

What we did to help ourselves.

We made a plan.

It's interesting that when armed with a pen and a sheet of paper one can feel so powerful. The electronic version is much the same—be it an Excel™ spreadsheet or a blank page in Word™.

Make a list and throw some dates beside the items and it becomes a lifeline. Pull up an email template and any number of wonderful people—on whose shoulders you can lean or cry—are a click away. Mouse to a spot on the tool-bar and the Mayo Clinic awaits your input, then delivers knowledge.

Three cheers for the mighty pen; ink or electronic. Both provide direction and hope (and write the words that become books).

Blindsided as we were, yes, we made a plan.

Our family is no different than yours in that we all have family and/or friends who have experienced cancer journeys. And so, because it worked for us as a coping strategy as well as organizing us, we'd highly recommend you make a list/plan too.

> **TASK/DRILL**: *Go to your local stationary store and purchase journals and binders; even a three-hole-punch or some 'punched' sheet protectors. The amount of information you'll receive through appointments, examinations, referral letters, and websites can be daunting. Being organized helps, allowing you to keep all the necessary information at your fingertips.*

Before every appointment we sat down and made a list of questions. This practice was invaluable.

We worked hard to remain balanced. Firm believers in being positive and realistic, we visited reputable websites and obtained information from medical professionals. And, because we believe in the power of complementary medicine we looked at a variety of trustworthy sources and remained open to whatever would create the best quality of life and offer positive healing results.

It's important to mention that it would have been easier to bury our heads in the sand, or even embrace a radical treatment that had no scientific proof, but we wanted to base all our decisions on professional advice backed by sound clinical evidence.

We aimed to create an inhospitable environment for cancer in any way we could. And we were certain that happiness played a part in that. Since Marnie thrived on family, flourished when involved in volunteer projects, and beamed when she participated in physical activities, we identified these 'sources' as a form of therapy in which she was already involved. Marnie's mood could be lifted the moment she spoke about a loved one, a project, or sports.

She was determined to remain strong for our children's events, and her curling. She did not stop volunteering or attending functions. Recognizing that 'doing what one loves is good medicine' was key to Marnie being able to remain strong. In turn that helped her find the energy and stability to assist in researching the disease in order to make informed decisions.

The ultimate part of her manifesto of healing was that she would not stop making the kids lunches. This latter point was her measuring stick—ours too.

What else did we do?

Well, we studied as if our lives depended on it, because our lives did.

It helped to know that it would take time to let the news sink in so that we could respond instead of react—at first it felt like alarm bells were continually going off in a 'do something now'. We regrouped.

We confided in trusted friends, and limited our time with those predisposed to drama.

In the eye of the storm, we put one foot in front of the other and combined our busy regular routine with a new schedule.

It was vital to keep 'normal' activities in our lives, but we knew that within the busy family schedule we had, we also had to make time for this imposter. We had to give it the royal treatment in understanding its pathology in order to physically and emotionally kick it out the door. This was draining, and it did take its toll some days.

When we made the decision for the double mastectomy (to minimize the chances of cancer coming back), we met with the plastic surgeon so that we could understand the process. Marnie's body resembled a road map after the doctor drew all over her, working to determine where he would remove fat in order to rebuild her breasts. Marnie, a small girl, did not have a lot to spare; therefore, the fat would have to come from many parts of her body. She was nervous, she was scared, and the staff understood that.

The one thing you will learn during a cancer journey is that no one is going to sugar coat anything. The explanations are thorough and can be quite graphic. This can shock you, especially if you're squeamish. But you need to get over this quickly so that you can be well prepared for all that's involved with the healing process as well as the possible outcomes.

We made ourselves aware and were prepared for every step. We knew the time required to heal or recover, how to manage the side effects, and what to do if there were changes to our plan.

Looking back, it's amusing to remember that Marnie was excited that her 'new boobs' would be smaller and perkier than her 'old ones'. However, this humour was contrasted by nervousness about how many people were going to see her naked.

Expect to ride the emotional waves that rise to humour and dip into despair. As a family: mom, dad, teenager, and preteen, our roles were well established; married for 19 years (at that point). We worked on our communication; mainly not being afraid to say the wrong thing to each other.

Sharing with our friends via one email was a huge time saver and massively cathartic. We positioned ourselves to use our energy to share but not feel burdened by the way others might handle our news. Basically, we had no expectations of others.

We knew that feedback would be based on the best each responder could do with the skills they had (based on his or her life experiences). And we prepared ourselves to answer from our authentic selves. 'Thank you for your kindness' or other short terms that were concise and loving were best because they were heartfelt.

One of the things that comes with a critical illness is that patients and families feel as though they've lost control. One feels powerless in an 'I can't do anything to change the situation'. This loss of control is one more 'stress' to add to a plethora of others. The emails we sent countered this; gave us something to do with the disease that we could 'own'. We could decide who we would tell, when we would tell them, and how.

In a short time, our family collectively went through a major growth spurt. We stepped up our game.

> *BRIAN: Everyone's experience differs in terms of the disease and response, but we all share a common bond: fear.*

> *When you first meet your medical team, things are quite formal. You will likely be very scared. You will probably have many questions and might not be sure how to go about asking them since it all seems so clinical and routine to everyone else. You might even think there are things you are supposed to know. And you will hear words that you have not heard before; might not know how to spell them in order to look up later.*

> *In addition, the examinations that are performed may seem extremely "by the book"; coldly so, with very straightforward commentary. Don't be frightened by this. These 'strangers in lab coats' will become your*

friends. They never lose their designations or their professionalism, but their guard eventually comes down, and you form a bond. A bond from a relationship you wish you'd never had to establish, but a bond nonetheless.

You will probably become frustrated by a multitude of vague descriptions, and it will drive you crazy hearing words or phrases like, "this may work", "we are unsure if", "it appears to be", or "we don't know if".

Cancer is not an exact science. This fact is what kept me up many nights.

As far as experiences: some respond to certain treatments and others don't, some get side effects and others escape these pleasantries. Some patients experience the placebo-result, defying previously chronicled results.

The professionals in this area can't predict what is going to happen; they are not treating a sprained ankle or broken arm. They are dealing with an inexact science, and work to do the best they can for each patient. Believe, have faith. This is truly a large part of your role.

What others did that was helpful.

They responded.

And there's a massive difference between reacting and responding. The emails we received were filled with love and kindness.

Sure, some people liked to recite their own journeys and experiences or offer a little advice. Having positioned ourselves from a place of having the energy to share but not feel burdened by the way others handled our news, we let the love flow in.

What others did that was helpful was to respond in love.

What the professionals did.

CancerCare Manitoba provided us with lots of information. The best resource that we drew from them was connected with their Patient Advocate Representative. An incredibly empathetic person—as are other reps—our advocate, Heather, helped us with the second opinion process. Heather, also my mother's name, guided us through the task of setting up an account at the Mayo clinic. She collected all the information required from the vast array of Marnie's tests, scans, and procedures, so we could package them for Minnesota. She reinforced that the chemo path we were on had been a viable option for many. She eased our emotional pain and made us feel like we were on the right path.

She was right: we were able to speak with an oncologist from the Mayo clinic who had reviewed Marnie's case history. Everything that was being done in Manitoba was, indeed, everything the Mayo Clinic would do. They recommended one more test, a PET scan, to confirm the diagnosis. This was a huge confidence booster for us.

It was helpful when staff explained procedures with pictures and diagrams, or suggested places we could go to read more about the topic they were covering.

The professionals demonstrated empathy and patience; a willingness 'not' to rush us through discussions. Using simple words or acronyms for the complicated, unpronounceable medical terms allowed us to comprehend the language of specialized medicine. They emphasized that there are no 'stupid' questions.

In addition, the professionals involved made us feel like we were all a team.

BRIAN: The staff's team aspect helped us bring the concept of team Marnie to our children. And since our children played sports, it was something tangible with which the kids could identify.

A couple of days after Marnie and I met with the breast reconstruction team, we headed to an education session to gather more information on the surgery we were facing. This was extremely informative as we learned what to do in order to support the surgery: how to get in and out of bed to avoid damaging the work that had been done; how to properly wrap the surgical area with tight 'binders' to help with healing; how to administer drugs to manage pain (and drugs to reduce the stress of bowel function); how to manage the patient at home.

I took notes the whole time while Marnie sat and listened; our usual approach. It helped me focus on the tasks and allowed Marnie to consciously slip away when she felt overwhelmed or scared. I highly recommend you assign someone to scribe at all meetings—please don't go alone to sessions and appointments.

I was the only man in a crowded room of women. There we all sat and learned, touching medical prostheses, compression bras, and foam pads. We were exposed to the world of areola tattooing and prosthetic nipples. We learned about possible risks associated with the surgery.

While driving home from this session we looked at each other and began to giggle, then broke out into full belly laughs. Marnie had always wanted a tattoo, but this was not what we expected. Again, our topics of conversation had certainly changed since the diagnosis, but our ability to find humour kept us sane.

THREE STARS

- Do not rush into anything; instant hospitalization is not usually required.
- Research from proven sources.
- Access your time-management skills. Find ways to free up time*.

*TIME SAVING EXAMPLES

- Setting up email lists so as not to have to type in individual names.
- Copy pasting material.
- Keeping the car gassed up.
- Tossing junk mail and unsubscribing from time-stealing mail.
- Hiring someone (if you can) to shovel the driveway or cut the lawn.
- Delegating tasks to family and friends.
- Saying YES to offers of help, and not feeling indebted to those helpers.

JUNIOR LEAGUE: MADISON (b. 1997)

When I was first told Mom had cancer I didn't really believe it. I was just in so much shock. There were so many emotions in my head that I couldn't even think, so I just cried.

I knew I needed to be strong and be there for my Mom. She was my best friend. It was my new reality, so I had to make the most of it.

At the time these questions popped up inside myself:
Were we going to lose our Mom?
Would she ever get better?
How are other people going to react?
Why did this happen to us? Why *my* Mom?

OVERTIME

http://www.bccancer.bc.ca/ This was our go-to site for reputable information

http://www.canadiancancertrials.ca/ We visited this weekly to see what new treatments were becoming available, and to see if we qualified for any trials. It allowed insight as to what was on the horizon for new treatments in Canada;

gave us hope that if we could hang on a little longer, new options would be available.

And this goes hand in heart with the A.A. Milne quote. **https://www.youtube.com/watch?v=9tRepZdoRmY)**

PLAYER PROFILE: MARNIE FOREMAN (taken directly and chronologically from the eulogy, and shared over the chapters of this book).

"Marnie and I almost never met. We were told a story at our Wedding by Marnie's (late) aunt Lauree (a story that neither of us knew). It was 1985, and I had just finished my first year of University. One of my teachers had asked that I come back and present some awards at the Provincial High School Fastball championships. At the awards ceremony I presented the MVP award to a person who was not there. As you probably have guessed, it was Marnie.

We did, however, meet many years later through Marnie's cousin, Martin. We were friends at first. We would run into each other at Jets games, socials, and the occasional bar. We talked about sports, her love for hockey and golf, (and) we spoke about travel, and her various trips through Europe. We talked about (the town of) Carman, and growing up in rural Manitoba. It was the beginning of a great relationship…"

Two

PLAY BY PLAY

January 22, 2013

Hello,

Please let me know if you do not want to receive updates. Again thanks to all of you for your kind letters, cards, e-mails, phone calls, and visits.

They all mean a lot to us and get us through the low parts of our days.

We want to update you on some news that we received today. Marnie has done a great job in preparing herself for her surgery date of January 28th. We have asked many questions, attended various seminars, and have read a lot of literature on the process that we *thought* we were going to experience. **Today all of this changed.**

This past seven days Marnie underwent many tests to prepare for her surgery. She completed her MUGA, CT, and bone scans last week. The results were very good for both the MUGA and bone scan. The results of the CT were not as clear and required us to have an MRI this past Monday to look at some of the findings.

This morning we received a call from our Oncology Surgeon to inform us that the abnormalities they found in the CT scan were indeed **cancer in the liver**. The feelings of anger, fear, and sadness from the initial breast cancer diagnosis were back. We all know that this disease is unpredictable, and can throw us many curveballs along the way. This news is shocking to us, but we continue to be positive as we await the next steps in this process.

So, what does this mean?

It means that they have cancelled Marnie's mastectomy surgery. We will seek advice from an oncologist, next week, to determine our course of chemotherapy. The surgeon says that this is a treatable disease and that chemotherapy could shrink and melt all of the tumors to prolong life for several years. It all depends on how Marnie's body reacts to therapy.

We continue to ask for your thoughts and prayers as we go through this together. Thanks again for all of your support; we cannot thank you enough for the love and kindness that has come through during this difficult time.

Brian, Marnie, Madison, and Brayden.

February 1, 2013

Hello Team Marnie,

It has been a little over a week since we communicated to you the latest news on Marnie's journey. It's amazing how many people have heard about her cancer and want to help in any way that they can. These acts of kindness add to our positive spirit and show us that we are truly blessed to have the friends and family that we do. It reminds us that we are not in this fight alone!

I was asked the other day how we could be so open about what Marnie and our family are going through. The answer is quite simple: communicating our journey is one of the only things we can control as we prepare for each day and the next step in this process. This disease turns your life upside down. It plays with your emotions: it makes you angry, sad, and scared. You become frustrated and impatient waiting for your results and your appointment dates. In essence, it consumes you 24/7.

Today, Marnie had yet another test. We made our way down to the Victoria Hospital to have the joyous experience of a colonoscopy. Results from her CT scan had shown some shading in a part of her bowel. For precautionary reasons they wanted to check this out and we are happy to report that this inflammation was not cancer, but a diagnosis of either ileitis, or Crohn's disease. This news on its own would normally be upsetting but, given the circumstances, we are relieved with the results.

Other than this procedure, this week was rather quiet as compared to weeks past. We have found out that we will be meeting with our oncologist, Dr. Marshall Pitz, on Tuesday February 5th. We are anxious to meet Dr. Pitz as we have heard very positive feedback about him (not just about his reputation as a doctor, but apparently he is quite the looker). This should make going to treatment much easier on Marnie and perhaps lead to a waiting list of drivers to take her to her chemo appointments! We are hoping this meeting will inform us of treatment options, and start dates.

The care we have received has been nothing short of amazing. The administration, nurses and physicians at Cancer Care do whatever it takes to accommodate requests and questions. They keep us informed and sane! We thank them for what they have done to date.

"Believe in yourselves and in everything that you are. Know that there is something inside of you that is greater than any obstacle" – Christian D. Larson (thank you Cathy J.).

Until next week…

Brian, Marnie, Madison, and Brayden

February 5, 2013

Hello Team Marnie,

We wanted to provide an update on our visit to CancerCare today and our appointment with Dr. Pitz. First of all, I am happy to report that there was no physical chemistry between Marnie and Dr. Pitz. To quote Marnie, "He is very cute, but not my type." I guess she prefers men who have a great face for radio.

Once again the staff at CancerCare continue to make us feel as comfortable as possible with their courteous, professional demeanor. Dr. Pitz went over our entire case file and answered all of the questions that have been on our mind for the past month. He displayed tremendous empathy as he summarized our journey to date, and our path forward. I will try to summarize what this will look like.

Dr. Pitz would like Marnie to have a portacath inserted in the right side of her upper chest so that the chemotherapy can be administered. This is done so that Marnie will not have to be poked by needles every time she goes for chemo, blood work, etc... They would like this to be done within the next seven days so they can start treatment. If they do not get the portacath done in time, Marnie will start chemo next week via the normal process of an I.V. in her hand. We hope that option #1 can be completed on schedule, as this allows us to have our chemo treatments at the Victoria Hospital (close to home). If not, we will have to start our treatments at CancerCare at Health Sciences Centre.

They have also ordered more tests. A PET scan and liver biopsy have been requested. We are awaiting word on dates for these procedures and will update you when we get more information.

Marnie's initial treatment will consist of a drug called Taxotere (Docetaxel). She will start with one treatment every three weeks. This will continue 4 times. After the fourth time, a CT scan will be performed to monitor drug performance and its effect on her cancer. Like many agents, there are side effects associated with treatment. While nausea and vomiting are not common with Taxotere, fatigue, muscle and joint pain, and hair loss are very common. Changes to, and loss of, finger nails can also result from this medication. We are not sure how many times she will have to complete this process or if she will stay on this medication. It all depends on how her body reacts to this form of chemotherapy.

As you can well imagine, all of this news today was a little overwhelming. But, Marnie was strong. She greeted Dr. Pitz in style by saying "it is not very nice to meet you" (tact has never been her strong suit), and proceeded to tell him that he needed to get this treatment going right away as she was tired of waiting (again, I refer to tact). This was all done in the first 10 seconds of meeting him! For those of you that know Marnie well, you should not be surprised.

Marnie continues to amaze me every day. Her display of inner strength through all of this is truly inspiring. While not without our moments of sadness, her positive, infectious attitude gets us through each day and prepares us for the challenges that lie ahead. I believe she draws this energy from her family and friends. We could not do this without all of you.
Take care.

Brian, Marnie, Madison and Brayden

TIME OUT

"It is much, much worse to receive bad news through the written word than by somebody simply telling you, and I'm sure you understand why. When somebody simply tells you bad news, you hear it once, and that's the end of it. But when bad news is written down, whether in a letter or a newspaper or on your arm in felt tip pen, each time you read it, you feel as if you are receiving the bad news again and again."

A SERIES OF UNFORTUNATE EVENTS — DANIEL HANDLER WRITING AS LEMONY SNICKET.

RECAP

News of the secondary cancer (liver) was like receiving an intentional hit from behind.

It took our breath away, and we thought we might have died a little bit that day—albeit temporarily. Author Daniel Handler, writing as Lemony Snicket, in his collection, *A Series of Unfortunate Events*, is correct: all the evidence surrounded us, on paper and in electronic form. Appointments on calendars, the emails we sent, and the comforting replies we received could, at times, feel like damning evidence; bad news redelivered. If only it could have all gone away with a return to sender. But it couldn't.

We were constantly reminded that this insipid disease was up-close and personal.

In effect, it was like starting again when we hadn't even really started handling things from the first round of bad news.

BRIAN:

Yes, of course, I ranted, mostly in the car, on a long run, or in the shower.

Treatable? Where the hell was the word curable?

There were dark moments.

I was sitting in Nicolino's restaurant with my boss when my cell phone rang. It was Marnie, and she was in tears trying to talk to me.

"Bri, it's not good, my MRI confirmed that the cancer has metastasized to my liver".

My heart dropped; more bad news. I left the restaurant and sped home. What do we do now? Is this treatable? What are our next steps? How do we tell the kids?

I cried most of the way home. I stopped in the driveway to compose myself; had to be calm for her.

Once inside, we discussed the call in great detail, then I called Dr. MacIntosh for confirmation of Marnie's account.

We were now dealing with an incurable cancer; one that could be controlled with current therapies, but never defined to be as "in remission". Dr. MacIntosh shared stories of patients who were still living years after this type of diagnosis.

She told me that every individual will have a different outcome based on how their body responds to treatment. Marnie and my goal remained the same as the first diagnosis: to beat it. The only thing that had changed was that now we were facing a tougher opponent.

COACH'S CORNER

What we did to help ourselves.

There are places to put those 'bad news' papers. Shredders, delete buttons, and files. It can feel healing to close a file folder, turn away, and order pizza. As well, there are other ways of looking at that paper: those hand written notes taken down during appointments, prescriptions, lab requisitions and results, evidence advances in science.

Caring notes are tactile tenderness—like receiving a hug. Paper trumps rock. And so we adjusted our attitude and caught our breath. Quite simply, for the sake of survival, we breathed life into each other.

We rallied.

And in the rallying department, no one rallied quite like the feisty red-head from Carman, Manitoba. We collected ourselves as if we were down by two in the final minutes of the third period. We were determined to meet the challenger head on; identify its collective weakness and overpower the opponent.

And we continued to help ourselves, even using our sense of humour, relying on it often. We knew we had to immerse ourselves in the language of medicine in order to prepare for meetings in which we'd ask questions, to keep up with myriad conversations with professionals, and in order to take in the information to come up with more questions. Yes, we trusted the professionals—and were in awe of their expertise—but that did not mean we could be complacent. Despite Heather Foreman's (Brian's mother) passing 19 years before, from cancer, there were terms, treatments, and branches of medicine we'd not heard of—technology and science advancements for which we were and continue to be grateful.

In terms of planning, though we were focused on time management, we knew we needed to build flexibility into the calendar. We were not robots; we needed scheduled timeouts. Additionally, having been blindsided by the additional diagnosis, on the heels of the first, we became aware that flexibility had to become our friend, for it was certain that a measure of unpredictability was to be expected; unexpected twists and turns—good or bad—are part of any journey.

On that note, and in hindsight, one thing that happened was that sometimes it seemed almost taboo to talk about the future. Everything was cancer centred and we were in survival mode. But, eventually, we carved out time to talk about what we'd like to do in terms of travel. And we set out some plans: a bucket list. Regardless of diagnosis, we'd recommend this for all those on a cancer journey—actually, on the life journey—because life is so precious, the planning and unfolding of dreams should be an exercise for everyone. We found it astonishing (when evaluating our pasts) to realize—even though we were an active family—that we only began to take our 'bucket list' seriously after the diagnosis.

What others did that was helpful.

They continued to respond. They asked for assignments.

Our friends were incredibly kind, but some confided guilt that they were glad it wasn't them. They, too, needed to forgive themselves for feeling that way—to recognize that 'being grateful it's not me' is normal—face it, none of us wants to find out they have cancer, or any other disease.

Close friends said they found it helpful to stop treading lightly around us, as if we were surrounded by broken glass. We found it helpful when our friends laughed and spoke about relevant things—an upcoming fundraiser, the volunteer list for a sports event, even the weather. This left it to us to bring up the topic of cancer.

Part of our management of the early part of the journey was to advise others of our progress. One email had led to another, and so on. While it meant that we needed to reply or at least express that we might not reply, we appreciated that people were great with whatever we did. And what they did to help—in addition to letting us take the lead in news-sharing—was they responded.

What the professionals did.

More than we could have imagined.

Our advocate was available and demonstrated total dedication to our well-being.

Doctors continued to educate us through talks, drawing diagrams, and providing links we could visit.

Nursing staff made us comfortable, be it a blanket or a smile.

Everyone involved in the journey knew their role and over-delivered in thoughtfulness and thoroughness.

THREE STARS

- Approach the paper/electronic trail with a positive attitude.
- Understand that the emotional ups and downs, in-house and externally, are normal and serve a purpose.

- Do not neglect talking about your dreams and making plans (no matter the size of those dreams and plans).

JUNIOR LEAGUE: BRAYDEN (b. 2001)

I couldn't believe it. I'd never thought this would ever happen to our family. I remember that right after Mom and Dad told us, the first thing I did was run downstairs to be alone—for two or three hours. It took me a couple of days to process what we'd learned about Mom. After that, it even took me a couple of months to get used to Mom being tired all the time. We definitely had to adjust to a new lifestyle.

I wondered if she'd be cured. How serious was the cancer? Would we lose her? What would other people think about this?

OVERTIME

http://www.cancer.net/navigating-cancer-care/cancer-basics

http://www.huffingtonpost.com/rayanne-thorn/mindfulness-practice_b_4026593.html

PLAYER PROFILE (taken directly and chronologically from the eulogy, and shared over the chapters of this book).

"You could say that we took the next step when, one evening, when I ran into her at a social at Sir John Franklin community center. We danced a little and said our goodnights.

Later that evening we accidently met up again at Winnipeg's Palomino Club. She was there for the music; I was there for the rum. One could say our relationship started when I grabbed the microphone and serenaded her to a Karaoke version of BTO's Taking Care of Business. "Handsome and talented"...she was hooked. I know that some of you in the room were there that day. The singing was awful, but she put up with me anyway.

We were engaged 6 months later, married 11 months after that, and happily married for over 22 years."

Three

INTERMISSION

Hello Reader:

Cancer does not discriminate; we're all in this together.

Not everyone who is diagnosed with cancer has a spouse or partner, a large network of friends, a family close by, nor might they have children.

Not everyone who is diagnosed with cancer has the financial means to leave his or her job, or is in a two income family that can rely on the income of one while the focus is on treatment and recovery.

Not everyone who is diagnosed with cancer lives in a city with a hospital— or if they do live in the city, the hospital is not always just around the corner.

Transportation to appointments comes with a price tag; and let's not forget the cost of hospital parking.

As certain chores become impossible, or household items require modification, life can become exhausting and expensive as myriad issues surface. Even items and services which will be reimbursed have to be paid for first, and that can severely affect cash flow or render the necessary 'item' or 'service' unattainable or undeliverable.

Everyone diagnosed with cancer deserves access to the best treatment and health care providers, and links to supportive people and networks that will understand their situation and champion their cause.

Everyone diagnosed with cancer needs as clear a view as possible to envision their future.

Ultimately, never has there been such a need to have supportive communities. And, on a personal level, a complete understanding of Mind, Body, and Soul.

Here are some best practices for those diagnosed with or directly affected by a cancer diagnosis:

- Breathe. No matter your circumstances, don't panic.
- Get ready to reach out and build a network.
- Take time for an overview of your situation.
- Share your fears.
- Make a list of questions related to your specific situation.
  How/when will I draft my team?
  How/when will I speak to my employer?
  What is my financial situation?
  What insurance coverage(s) do I have?

Specifically:

When you draft your team, evaluate who is in the best position to be present and aware of all the circumstances at all times. Someone who is along for the whole journey so that they can take on the responsibility of knowing the situation and communicating it to others. In our case, Marnie had the diagnosis, and Brian (spouse, Dad) took on the notetaking and communication (not that Marnie wasn't involved). Others helped with food and transportation. There were a variety of things we didn't even know we needed, but as we moved through the process, we discovered and asked. Likewise, others helped us understand what might make life easier, and then volunteered to provide those things.

Employment:

If you are the one diagnosed with cancer:

1) If you work for a large company, the Employee Assistance Program, accessed through the HR department, will be able to advise you and liaise with your supervisor or management.
2) If you work for a Mom and Pop operation then a proactive discussion with the owners is required.
3) If you *are* the Mom and Pop operation, then look for resources available to the self-employed—the UK has a small PDF which contains some basic information which overviews various situations (if your computer does not allow the automatic download of this PDF, go to Macmillan.org and click on resources for the handbook):

http://www.macmillan.org.uk/documents/cancerinfo/selfemploymentbooklet.pdf

In Canada, help may be available through various insuring agencies:

http://www.cancer.ca/en/cancer-information/cancer-journey/living-with-cancer/dealing-with-change/changes-to-finances/?region=on

If a family member has been diagnosed:

1) Inform your employer about your situation.
2) Set up reasonable expectations as to the time required to be a caregiver.

BRIAN: *In my case, I could not have asked for better support from my employer and my boss. All were incredibly empathetic of our situation. I was harder on myself with my own work expectation than they were.*

3) Update your supervisors/managers/staff regularly. Don't assume they know what is going on. Set up monthly touch points with the appropriate people to explain what has happened, and what is to come.

4) Know what resources are there for you from an employee perspective. What are their specifics as to allowing time off? What are your benefits for medications? Do they cover massage or reflexology therapy? What about acupuncture? Does your plan involve wig coverage? What does your out of country travel insurance look like? Do you have an Employee Assistance Program? How do you access it? These are all good things to know that can help your peace of mind as you go through treatment.

If you are alone and feel you do not have a network:

1) It's essential you let your doctor know that you are alone. No one should go solo on a cancer journey. The medical professionals involved may be able to offer a community link for you to access.

2) Consider contacting a cancer care advocate through your local cancer center.

3) Talk to someone who has been through it. A friend or a friend of a friend.

There are also ways to get connected with other patients. http://cancerhopenetwork. org/get-support/get-matched/with-a-cancer-survivor.html

If you are concerned about transportation:

Once you've identified a network of people who might assist you, utilize the network and never be afraid or ashamed to ask for help.

1) The Canadian Cancer Society has a division which assists with transport through volunteer drivers and transit systems.
2) Reach out to various groups, including faith based groups—many people do not realize, for example, that Catholic Family Services serves all and does not require those they serve (or who volunteer) to be of Catholic faith. Most faith-based groups have a non-denominational policy.

If you are retired and on a fixed income:

Some of the above points will come into play—your level of insurance, your network of people, and the amount of direction and assistance from the medical professionals in your life. It is essential to:

1) Identify a trusted friend or family member to organize a network/ team around you. Have that person as your 'team leader'.
2) Not be afraid of asking for help.
3) Locate a seniors group and/or an advocate.
4) Not be shy about asking for answers to be repeated, written, or explained further with links and pictures.
5) Speak (or ask your team-leader to speak on your behalf) to employees in the departments of provincial and federal government agencies regarding benefits and insurance.
6) Become somewhat internet savvy; it may be time to get a quick tutorial so that you can access myriad links (and save time on the phone).

If children are involved: *see story on how we told our children.* *

1) If they're young (under 8) 'not too much detail' advises the American Cancer Society. Besides, you may not have all the information, initially.
2) Definitely, at any age (including for some children under 8), name of the cancer, the body part which is affected, how it will be treated, and how the child's day-to-day life might change.

3) An excellent link covers more (turn the printer on and get those binders opened):

http://www.cancer.org/treatment/childrenandcancer/helping-childrenwhenafamilymemberhascancer/dealingwithdiagnosis/dealing-with-diagnosis-how-to-tell-children

In summary, breathing is beneficial. Don't try to do everything at once. Use this list as a guide, then take action and begin to cross some things off. Breathe.

How we told our children*

BRIAN: When we first received news of the diagnosis our first reaction was, "How the hell do we tell the kids?"

We became very emotional as we discussed the many ways we wanted this to happen. In the end we made the decision to be honest, and not delay telling them. There are too many ways that people can get their information. Social media is rampant with news. If they were going to hear anything about their mom it was going to be from us and it was going to be the truth. This had to be one of the toughest things that we have ever had to do.

How do you tell a child that his or her mom has cancer? We sat Madison (15) and Brayden (11) on the sofa and told them everything that we had gone through to date: Marnie's diagnosis, and—as far as we knew—what to expect.

There were tears, there were hugs, there were many questions, but most of all there was unity.

It was clear from the start that they were in this with us and would do anything to support their mom.

The unknown is scary. We had no idea how they would respond. We didn't know if it would impact their schoolwork. Neither did they. Would their friends still want to come by the house and visit? How might the children react when their mom lost her hair or couldn't get out of bed for a couple of days? We had no idea what went through—or would go through—their minds.

But, we made time for them to ask questions, and we explained the next procedure and test that was going to happen. We kept them educated. I was amazed at the compassion and maturity that Madison and Brayden demonstrated, and the resiliency they built along the way. TRUST YOUR CHILDREN.

Hold them, hug them, trust them.

SPECIFIC TO CAREGIVERS

A Caregiver goes through many emotions when supporting a loved one.

BRIAN: I was no different.

Why the hell did this disease choose us? We are good people, we volunteer, obey the law, donate to charity, and are kind to others. But cancer shows no mercy. I had to face it: there are no merit points given for service to others in order to escape cancer's grasp.

There are many things that a cancer patient doesn't need to hear from the caregiver. The circle of 'ranting' or 'commentary' needs to go outward to friends and professionals, not inward to the person at the centre of the issue. After all, they're dealing with their own brand of guilt and concern.

When someone uses that phrase 'make sure the caregiver takes care of themselves' it is a reflection of the importance of the well-being of the caregiver. There is nothing selfish about this concept. It's essential to have a support system that helps the primary caregiver. Most often, caregivers don't understand this concept because they're not the ones who are 'suffering', 'terminal', 'critical', or 'in need'. But all of these terms can apply to a caregiver.

In my case, I was fortunate. Marnie had so much support from various communities because she'd been so active in those same communities. Often, they directed me. As well as family, we had helpers at the ready. Yet even with that support for which I am thoroughly grateful—my role was the primary one. And, as the frontline caregiver, the need to protect, feed, clothe, soothe, and shoulder responsibilities began to take its toll.

I want to share personal observations of a few of the tougher aspects which can be easily overshadowed by the crisis at hand. Simply being aware that other caregivers experience these feelings is helpful in the 'I'm not alone' department. In addition, knowing how certain things affected me will help someone else circumvent issues or at least navigate them.

- *I had trouble concentrating, and I started to forget things at work. As well, simple arrangements in the children's schedules seemed difficult to keep track of. It became imperative I write everything down, not just medical notes.*

- *I got mad when close friends ignored us. And I kept those feelings to myself. Yes, we had many friends who stuck by us, but we had others who did not. In the thick of things I couldn't think of any reason they'd do this and I experienced anger and frustration; I was upset with them. "How the heck could they turn their backs on us when we needed them the most?" This anger slowly turned to a feeling of loneliness; even abandonment. When a number of emotions (in this category) ran through my system I had all kinds of thoughts about what to do: should I call them and voice my frustration? Not call them—after all, where had they been the last two months?*

  Eventually, though, what I realized is that no one had intentionally chosen to leave us out in the cold. Certain people did not know how to deal with the situation. Some didn't know how to behave when they were around us. Others weren't sure what they should say when they saw us.

  What I needed to do was develop a swift process for forgiveness so as not to let this drive me crazy. And I did. I advise calm waters and a forgiving attitude; there's simply too much other stuff to deal with.

- *I saw the dark side. Cancer can lead a person there. It's not difficult to cross the line and become negative. Cancer forces people to think about the 'what ifs'.*

  What if this treatment doesn't go well?
  What if the side effects are too hard to manage?
  What if Brayden and Madison can't handle seeing their mom being sick?

What if I can't be a caregiver and work, then have to quit my job?
What if she doesn't make it and I lose my soul mate?
How would I manage being a single parent? Children do not come with
a self-training manual: sons and daughters need specific role models.

These are all realistic scenarios, and yet they have an edge to them that goes beyond practical planning for the future. I had to work extremely hard to push the challenging questions out of the way and focus on the now.

Making a bit of a list in my head, and getting in the habit of doing that—basically a gratitude list—helped me push through the negatives. When I caught myself heading toward the road of 'what ifs', I'd do my best to U-turn and head down gratitude lane.

I was grateful for the love and support the surrounded us; for those good friends that provided us their shoulders every step of the way; for sports and that participating or spectating provided a great distraction. Gratitude allowed me to get to a place of hope; hope that what we were doing was going to work. I knew my energy was best used to help lead our family spirit so we could put our efforts into helping Marnie get better.

Caregivers, PLEASE identify whatever you need to remain healthy and clear minded, then take action to ensure you *are* healthy on *all* levels.

Four

PLAY BY PLAY

February 13, 2013

Hello Team Marnie,

> *"Patience and perseverance have a magical effect before*
> *which difficulties disappear and obstacles vanish."*

— JOHN QUINCY ADAMS

Another whirlwind week behind us! In the last update we informed you that we were waiting for Marnie to have a portacath surgically placed in the upper right chest area in order to receive her chemo treatments. The benefit of having this is that they will not have to use the veins in her hands or arms (Marnie has small veins and they have trouble finding them for needle insertion) for chemo or blood work. All can be done through the portacath. Many of you have asked what a portacath is. Well here is an attempt at an explanation...

According to Dr. Google... "A small medical device that is installed beneath the skin. It contains a catheter that connects the port to a vein (in Marnie's case, the superior vena cava). This allows drugs to be injected and blood samples to be drawn many times." It is about the size of a toonie.*

The benefit of being connected to the superior vena cava (Just up from the right atrium) is that drugs will spread throughout the body quickly and efficiently once administered.

Of course this could not be done without a story; as of Thursday of last week we had not heard from CancerCare as to a surgery date for the port. We were wanting to have this done as soon as possible to avoid some of the side effects of chemo treatment (skin burning and irritation) as well as the convenience of having her first chemo treatment done at the Victoria Hospital.

In taking matters in our own hands, and through a family friend, we were able to obtain a consult with a surgeon, last Friday, in Portage La Prairie. The meeting with the surgeon was brief and Marnie, questioning the proficiency of a small town surgeon, asked a couple of poignant questions... "Have you ever done this surgery before?", and then followed up with, "are you any good at it?" I think this shocked the surgeon, but thank goodness the answer to both queries was "yes".

We're happy to report that the procedure was done on Monday without incident.

Marnie has been quite sore in the surgery area, but appears to be getting more pain-free with each passing day. Thank you to both Dr. Parker (no relation) and Dr. Ross for helping us through this on short notice. On Tuesday we met with the family physician oncologist Dr. Chris Ogaranko who will be supervising our chemo treatments at the Victoria Hospital. Dr. Ogaranko works closely with Dr. Pitz and facilitates the chemo process so we are able to have it done at a more convenient location. We once again went over our diagnosis, treatment, and post chemo medications that will help to fight infection and nausea. Today, we were back at the Victoria Hospital for a successful test of the portacath (the wonders of small town medicine!) and to meet our chemo therapy nurses.

So…we had done all of our homework, prepared for the treatment, met our support team, and were ready to start chemo on Thursday, but we were informed on Tuesday that we needed to have another test done.

Through our journey, we have had the opportunity to consult with an oncologist at the Mayo clinic. He was happy with the advice, care, and process that we have been going through, but suggested that we ask for a PET scan. A PET scan can bring a number of benefits to cancer assessment and care. They can reveal images that might not show up on a CT scan, MRI, or x-ray. It can show the extent of the disease, help determine if and where the cancer has spread, and can help our physician monitor disease size/recurrence and show the effectiveness of therapy. The PET scan cannot be done close to chemo therapy as it skews the results of the test. At our request, CancerCare has made arrangements for us to have this scan done on Friday.

Next steps…our chemo adventure starts on Tuesday morning. Marnie will undergo her first infusion treatment at 10:00 AM. We are anxious to get started, and realize that the road ahead may be bumpy but the end result will be well worth it!

Thanks again for all of your love and support. It helps us through the bad times and makes us look forward to the good times that lie ahead.
Until our next update…

Brian, Marnie, Madison, and Brayden

February 22, 2013

Hello Team Marnie,

It's hard to believe that another week has flown by. We had our PET Scan last Friday and filled the rest of the weekend running errands. We are still waiting to hear the results from this test.

One of the highlights of the week was securing a wig for Marnie. Hair loss change will be emotional for her, and finding a wig that makes her feel comfortable and confident was essential to us. I had the unique experience of accompanying Marnie on one of these shopping excursions. Many questions were asked that day…

"Do we go with synthetic, or real hair?" "Do I go with one with bangs?" "Can these be coloured, cut, combed, straightened, or washed?"

I don't know who was more flustered, me or Marnie. If anyone has seen my hair, they would soon realize that having me provide input on this decision would be like asking Van Gough about earmuffs! Happy to report that it all turned out great; all of Marnie's objectives were met. The wig she picked out is perfect and, well, looks like MARNIE.

Thank you, Tammie D., for your compassion, patience, understanding, and mostly your friendship through this process. We truly are grateful.

Acts of kindness come when you least expect. I had planned to cut my hair very short to show support for Marnie (I know…insert joke here). What we did not know is that others were with us. Some of the Dads from Brady's hockey team got together on Saturday night for an impromptu shaving. An *awesome* display! Thanks guys—we are humbled by your actions.

A special thanks to Paolo and Vicki S., and Bill L. Your generosity certainly touched our hearts. We hear that others may be following this trend. Stay tuned…We also want to send a special "shout out" to Mark E. Your advice, guidance, and support have been invaluable. Words of appreciation are not enough, but thank you.

Well, we officially started our chemotherapy on Tuesday at the Victoria Hospital. While we were looking forward to getting our treatment started, it was a day that brought back many memories for us. Upon arrival we were led to a room that was dedicated in my mother's name. How perfect and appropriate that we begin this challenge knowing the courage and strength of Heather Foreman is with us.

Marnie did awesome, and the infusion went as smooth as possible. She went home feeling great and ready for the side effects that accompany treatment.

Wednesday and Thursday went well. No changes were seen. These days were filled with watching curling, and the occasional outing with her parents (Wal-Mart, Costco, and of course a trip to check out the deals at the soon to be closed Zellers). She also made it out to a jewelry party on Thursday evening!

Later Thursday night, and throughout today, Marnie started experiencing the achiness and joint pain associated with Taxotere treatment. This is quite common and usually lasts 2-4 days. She is also beginning to feel quite tired. Thanks to some good pharmacotherapy, we have not seen any signs of nausea.

Next week is when her white blood cells, and hence her immune system, will be at their lowest. This will cause Marnie to, again, experience fatigue. She should start to bounce back with more energy toward the weekend. No doubt that she will continue to approach all challenges with the incredible strength and determination she has demonstrated thus far.

"In everyone's life, at some time, our inner fire goes out. It is then burst into flame by an encounter with another human being. We should all be thankful for those people who rekindle the inner spirit."

ALBERT SCHWEITZER

I saw this quote and it reminded us of the tremendous support we have received from our friends, family, colleagues, and the community. We are blessed to be surrounded by you all and continue to gain our strength from your positive energy.

Until the next update…

Brian, Marnie, Madison, and Brayden

March 8, 2013

Hello Team Marnie,

An update on Marnie's Journey over the last couple of weeks...Wow, we continue to be amazed by the support from all of you! Team Marnie continues to grow on a daily basis as more people are discovering her diagnosis and are looking for ways to help us fight this disease and raise awareness (and funds) for cancer. Absolutely amazing...

Marnie's response to her first chemo treatment went exactly as predicted. In our last communication we commented that she was feeling good, but experiencing some joint pain. This pain continued for a couple of days and then was accompanied by a period of extreme fatigue (as her immune system was at its lowest). It was great to see by the end of the week that she was gaining her energy back; she even attended Brayden's hockey game last Friday evening. She is feeling great right now and is ready for round two starting next Wednesday.

Thanks to all of the families who provided meals and treats. We cannot begin to tell you how much this is appreciated during these hectic times.

On Wednesday of this week we received the findings of Marnie's PET scan. This is a more accurate test to determine the location and progression of the cancer. The results confirmed what we have learned to date: breast cancer and breast cancer that has metastasized to the liver. They still would like to perform a liver biopsy for a 100% disease confirmation. We are awaiting word on a date for this procedure. While we were hoping for different results, we continue to be optimistic and remain vigilant in our fight.

Creating a buzz for Marnie...

More people have stepped up and joined the trend to support Marnie and her fight against cancer. There was yet another head shaving event at Escape Hair (a rather appropriate name) – Great work Paolo!

Thanks Brent F., Troy H., Brent O., and Trevor J. for the support...looks great on you. A huge thanks to Bruce M., whose "Buzzing it off for Marnie" campaign raised over $8,000.00 for CancerCare Manitoba. Truly great stuff...

Encouragement never seems to be in short supply. Good friends of ours are in Tampa Bay for an "old timers" (sorry guys) hockey tournament and attended the Jet's vs Lightning game last night.

Our gratitude goes out to Scott L., Chris D., Derrick M., and Kent M. "Team Marnie" has gone global, as they created a "Fight Like a Girl Banner" that was proudly displayed with them inside the Tampa Bay arena.

Wednesday was perhaps the most emotional day we have faced thus far. Marnie had begun to experience hair loss throughout last weekend and it rapidly progressed throughout the week. She made the decision to call her friend Tammie to cut off her remaining hair.

This experience was humbling in so many ways. I witnessed the power of friendship from Tammie, the sincerity, and compassion from our daughter Madison, as she helped to cut her mom's hair (we are donating her pig tails to help make a wig), and the courage Marnie displayed throughout the process.

I know that she feels weird, and self-conscious about her new look, but I can tell you that she looks beautiful and that bravery never goes out of fashion! Love you all!

Until the next update...

Brian, Marnie, Madison, and Brayden

TIME OUT

"It doesn't happen all at once," he said. "You become. It takes a long time. That's why it doesn't often happen to people who break easily, or have sharp edges, or who have to be carefully kept. Generally, by the time you are Real, most of your hair has been loved off, and your eyes drop out and you get loose in the joints and very shabby. But these things don't matter at all, because once you are Real you can't be ugly, except to people who don't understand."

THE SKIN HORSE FROM THE VELVETEEN RABBIT — MARGERY WILLIAMS

RECAP

We became more real. We didn't break easily. Of course, we wouldn't have chosen this path or wish it upon anyone, but once on it, we chose the way we marched over the rough patches and lingered in the nicer spots.

We took cover under a large umbrella of connection, family and friendship; essentially we were protected by love.

Looking back, what we didn't realize at the time was that, within the safety of a team, we were able to totally experience unconditional love by feeling free enough to be miserable; safe enough to have heavily charged disagreements; and generally okay when we expressed frustration. This freedom of expression served to strengthen our relationship.

BRIAN: I got over feeling sorry for Marnie and for myself; one can't be productive while tangled in pity. While it might sound odd to hear advice like 'be yourself' (after all, who else can you be?), a diagnosis does challenge the natural flow. If having the occasional argument, whining about spilled juice, or needing quiet time were the norm for you before the diagnosis, then don't feel like you have to stop doing or feeling stuff that is normal for you. There'll be enough changes. By all means, dig deep and find the best that is you, but don't walk on eggshells around your family, and especially not around yourself.

I used my alone-time in my car to express my frustrations. This seemed to be the best time to let go of my emotions. I did not want my kids to see how I was feeling, or to recognize panic or worry on my face. I would turn the radio up and scream and swear at the top of my lungs. This was also my time to cry. I'm sure there were many drivers who pulled up beside me wondering what the heck was going on, and who the lunatic was beside them.

As you move forward, take great consideration to 'choose and make' time to be with your loved one (without the cancer in the room). Yes, cancer consumes days and nights, and yes, cancer's serious 'business', but we drew strict boundaries for timeouts. We made time for 'meetings' where we discussed certain aspects—almost businesslike. And we carved out time to 'not' discuss cancer. In doing that, we put cancer in its place instead of it ruling our schedule.

COACH'S CORNER

What we did to help ourselves.

Use your network: your family doctor, your friends, and their friends, basically everyone possible to get everything you 'need' done. While there are many great doctors and nurses that help along the way, you need to be in control of your journey. Own it.

When we found out that Marnie's disease had progressed and she needed a port inserted to initiate chemotherapy this is exactly what we did.

BRIAN: I am fortunate to work in the healthcare industry, and like to think I have an understanding of the administrative side to our business, but nothing I've done in my professional life could prepare me for what we were to go through.

As much as you study the surgeries, how to be a caregiver, the medications, schedules, and side-effect management, you need to understand your healthcare system.

You and your team need to know the people and places to contact when you have questions, when you need something urgently, or, where/when a fever spikes or there's uncommon reaction to treatment. You and your team need to be one step ahead of the process and be prepared to expect the unexpected, then face it.

But the hardest thing you will need to learn is to be forceful. You will have to come to terms with sometimes going beyond being a strong advocate, and let the 'worries' about 'pissing people off' fall to the wayside. You will need to ask for things—though politely and diplomatically—that you would not typically ask for (and that might feel awkward, weak, or selfish). Please remember, you are not dealing with a skinned knee; this is a time when you are the priority.

Ironically, through a friend of a hockey player I'd coached decades before, we made contact with someone who could help. Ken was now a doctor in rural Manitoba, and had connections to a surgeon. The wait in the city of Winnipeg was too long, and we wanted to start chemo as soon as possible. We spoke on Thursday afternoon, had a consult on Friday, and the port was installed the following Monday. It may not seem like much, but this small victory allowed us to feel that we were proactive in attacking the disease.

Purely from a mental perspective it felt like we were able get in the game earlier to battle this much larger opponent.

Administrative activities, advocating, and generally staying as on top of things as one can, makes a big difference to one's spirits.

We stress again, if you have not started a file system/note-taking habits, do so now. It saves time, it soothes, it pays off in so many ways.

Documenting the journey—without sometimes knowing we were, like in the emails to others—was one of the most valuable assets we had. It made the cancer journey a business (helpful when dealing with some aspects), and yet it was therapeutic also.

If you cannot make notes (or do not have a team member who will attend appointments with you) then use the recording device on your smartphone or pick up a digital recorder, then transpose later. The key is to file each piece of paper and write or record every bit of information.

In the helping ourselves category, pre-planning involved anticipating needing a wig, then trying to find the perfect one. Marnie wanted one that would make her feel like, well, herself.

> BRIAN: *The search for wigs was endless. We visited many local shops, took a trip across the border to Grand Forks, North Dakota, and spent countless hours online trying to locate the 'one'.*

> *On one occasion I accompanied the crew—Marnie, Madison and our close friend, Tammie, to a local wig store. While Marnie was quite serious about the selection process, Madison and I went off to see what best suited*

our personalities. I took on many identities that day: from Bette Midler to the Hanson Brothers of the movie Slapshot. We had many laughs. It's hard to believe that Marnie never invited me back on another hair finding adventure.

And so it was, on a cold winter day, Marnie, Madison, and our close friend, Tammie, drove to a shop in rural Manitoba—without me—to check out the selection.

They were greeted by a lovely lady who ran a home business. Kind and caring for certain, she was slightly unconventional; perhaps some would say eccentric. The thing is, this caring lady loved cats and her home was filled with them. The other thing is: Marnie hated cats!

Apparently they shopped while playing feline hopscotch, and like in all stories that contain houses of cats and eccentric ladies, it was magical. Yes! They found two more-than-excellent choices—whodathunkit? The wigs were exact matches to Marnie's ginger tones. The first one was made from natural hair and the other was synthetic. She so appreciated that this lady had set up a business that included helping those who needed a wig, but it didn't stop us from a 'little' teasing about ginger cat hair.

All kidding aside, we were grateful for this 'home business'. I'll not forget the expression of relief on Marnie's face that evening as she brought her wigs home and modeled them for us. She'd never wanted to wear a bandana as she thought that others would judge her as 'being sick'. These new looks brought back a sense of confidence that we'd not seen in a while; her smile proved it.

If you're looking for a wig, your local chapter of 'CancerCare' can point you in the right direction. They have many pieces that are available free of charge. You may also find that they provide make-up services and beauty tips for cancer patients; a nice resource offered to make you feel a bit more like yourself.

We mentioned earlier that we did a lot of shopping on line. While there are many excellent sites, the one that we used was www.wigsalon.com

Upon Marnie's passing, we donated all of her wigs to CancerCare Manitoba. We hope that the person or people who inherited them gleaned as much positivity from them as Marnie did.

And there's more hair to come: one of we three is currently growing out (her) hair; intending to donate it to help make a wig for another patient.

> *On June 1, 2016 Madison made the courageous decision to cut her long hair and donate it to help make a wig for another patient.*

What others did that was helpful.

The moms on Brady's hockey team organized a web based 'Meal Train' where community friends and hockey parents took the time to cook and deliver meals to our home. Appreciated on so many levels, it allowed us down-time after chemotherapy, and we were able to look after Marnie as she experienced the fatigue and side effects of those first treatments, and dealt with the anxiety that accompanied them.

We are not an easy family to cook for as Brayden has celiac disease, hence a gluten free menu was required. But people took the time out to understand the dietary requirements—including many upgrades we chose in order to provide better nutrition.

Our association with organizations and teams provided moral support, too. A funny story: when Brayden's hockey team was in their Minor Peewee playoff run, the hockey moms would show their support by wearing the spare team jerseys as they cheered on our boys. However, this overlapped with Marnie's first days with her wig—and as it was such a close match to her own hair, some didn't know she wore one. After a particular game, as the moms were helping each other to get the jerseys off each other's heads, Marnie's red wig almost accompanied the shirts into the jersey bag. Marnie's quick reflexes helped to maintain decorum and avoid an awkward situation.

What the professionals did.

CancerCare Manitoba provided us with a lot of useful information. They have a great website that covers many topics. Other provinces likely have similar links.

Their connection to a Patient Advocate Representative is invaluable. These reps are incredibly empathetic people who can help you navigate your cancer journey. Ours, Heather—mentioned earlier—guided us through a forest of paper. Empathetic and well informed, she was a skilled listener and always had a shoulder on which we could lean.

Another positive, through the professionals in our lives, came via speaking with an oncologist from the Mayo clinic who had reviewed Marnie's case history. As mentioned in the email, the clinic's information aligned with what was being done in our Province.

In summary we found support through various professional links and referrals. Awareness—simply of their existence—helped a great deal, as we learned how overwhelming such a large network of technologists and clinicians could seem.

> *BRIAN: And it was good that we were buoyed with positives, because our first chemo experience was daunting. I remember walking into the Victoria Hospital with huge optimism. We were going to do this.*
>
> *Now, I have played in many hockey games, in many arenas, and in front of many people, but this venue scared the crap out of me.*

But, as they placed us in our treatment room, that very room dedicated to my mother, Heather Foreman, we did not feel alone. We then met our nurses; more angels. They held Marnie's hand, they gave her a warm blanket when she was cold, and educated her as to everything that was going to happen to her that day. They cared. None of the staff knew, at the time, our connection to the room.

What does a portacath look like? http://www.cancer.ca/en/cancer-information/diagnosis-and-treatment/tests-and-procedures/subcutaneous-port/?region=on

THREE STARS

- Study your healthcare system and patient care process as much as you research your treatment process.
- Talk to people about next steps even though you may be unsure of your course of action.
- Do not stop taking notes. Keep your file system up to date.

JUNIOR LEAGUE: BRAYDEN

Every morning, before school, she would (try to) wake me up at 7:15, and she would keep yelling at me until I actually got out of bed. Since it was so early in the morning I didn't always get up right away, so she'd go back and forth, doing stuff then returning, trying to wake me up again. Time after time. And, I'd say, "Yes, I'm awake, I'm up," but when she'd leave I'd fall back asleep. Still, she just kept it up until I was!

OVERTIME

Links from the UK, USA, and Canada that deal with the side effects of chemotherapy.

http://www.breastcancer.org/tips/hair_skin_nails/wigs

http://www.cancerresearchuk.org/about-cancer/coping-with-cancer/
coping-physically/changes-to-your-appearance-due-to-cancer/hair-loss/
coping-with-hair-loss

https://www.cancer.ca/en/support-and-services/support-services/
hair-donations/?region=on

PLAYER PROFILE (taken directly and chronologically from the eulogy and shared over the chapters of this book).

"When we first started seeing each other there were two words that (when written together) *I despised. COUNTRY MUSIC.*

I was a city boy who liked The Tragically Hip, U2, and ACDC. I thought Garth Brooks was a stream near her home town, and could not understand why anyone would want to go "fishing in the dark". She slowly converted me. QX104 became a staple on our radio dial and soon took over from my traditional tastes.

She loved Reba McIntyre, Carrie Underwood, Keith Urban, Tim McGraw, Faith Hill, and really anything country. She led the line dance at socials, bars, and parties whenever Brooks and Dunn's Boot Scootin' Boogie was on.

She taught me to two-step. It was in her soul. Last summer (2014) we were able to share this love with our kids as we attended The Zac Brown Concert at Investors Group Stadium.

We sang, and danced; we enjoyed the August evening. It is something she loved and I am happy that she had made this a part of our lives."

Five

PLAY BY PLAY

March 15, 2013

Hello Team Marnie,

> *"Courage is not the absence of fear, but*
> *rather the judgement that something*
> *else is more important than fear."*
>
> (James Neil Hollingworth writing under
> the penname of Ambrose Redmoon.)

I saw this quote and it reminded me of something that happened recently in our home. We realized that Marnie's hair loss would be tough for her, but what we did not fully understand was how this would affect our eleven year old son, Brayden. Since last Wednesday he was having a very hard time with his mom shaving her head and did not want to see her this way. In his own words, "I am not ready yet."

This led to an interesting pattern of events with Marnie rushing to put on a hat or her wig every time Brady was around. This past weekend Brayden woke up very early and came into our room and Marnie jumped up and ran to get a hat on. Brayden stopped her and told her that "it is okay" and

---

announced that "I am ready now." He met his mom with a hug and a smile and continued on with his day.

In true Brady fashion, it just had to be on his terms. We tend to focus on the bigger issues when we go through a challenge like this, and sometimes forget how this can impact others in our lives. The courage our kids have displayed to manage change has been nothing short of amazing. Whether it has been Madison helping to cut her mom's hair or Brady giving mom the thumbs up on her new hat purchases helps us to realize that they are invested in this battle as much as we are. We are truly blessed.

On Monday this week we went to the Victoria hospital to have blood work done and to meet with Dr. Ogaranko. Marnie's blood levels were very good. Normal white cell count is eleven, and hers were above thirteen. This puts her in a good place to fight infection and to continue to her next round of chemotherapy. We also learned from Dr. Ogaranko that her breast cancer was not HER2-positive.

This was very good news as HER2-positive breast cancers tend to be more aggressive than other types of breast cancer and would have required other drugs being added to her current therapy. We had been awaiting news on this test from Marnie's initial breast and lymph node biopsy back in November. The reason you have to wait so long for the results is that this test has to be sent away to Toronto and there is usually a backlog there. The good news is that our local government has now purchased equipment to process these tests so the results will be available much quicker for Manitoba residents.

Wednesday brought about Marnie's second round of chemotherapy. We arrived at the hospital at 10:00 AM and finished treatment around noon. All went as good as can be expected. I know we have mentioned this before, but the nurses at the Victoria Hospital are second to none. What they do for their patients on a daily basis is heroic. Thanks to Cathy, Claudette, and Delleen for your empathy, understanding, and fabulous sense of humour.

As with the first treatment, Marnie is feeling very good. She was able to attend a couple of Brady's hockey games and a Driver's Ed meeting for Madison (hard to believe she will be on the road soon). While we expect the side effects to hit her soon, we are better prepared to handle them this time around. Thanks for your continued thoughts and prayers.

Until the next update…

Brian, Marnie, Madison, and Brayden…

April 5, 2013

Hello Team Marnie,

Hope everyone had a great spring break. It is shocking to see how much snow is still on the ground in Winnipeg. We are sure in for a long wet April/ May… Wanted to provide you all with an update on Marnie's journey.

So…

We managed the side effects of chemotherapy much better the second time around, and Marnie was able to attend all of Brayden's final hockey playoff series (lost in game 5 of a best of 5 series).

Pain from the Taxotere treatments was not nearly as bad as round one, but fatigue seemed to last a little longer. This was and still has been accompanied by a wicked cold complete with a bad cough, a stuffy nose and plugged ears. It seems to be getting better slowly with each passing day.

As many of you have already guessed, we use and draw a lot of parallels and inspiration from adages and quotes we are sent, and have found, throughout this process.

This edition will be no different...

"I didn't want normal until I didn't have it anymore".

— Maggie Stiefvater, Lament: The Faerie Queen's Deception.

To say that we are a busy family would be an understatement. Our chosen lifestyle is one of chaos. This, like many of your lives, is **OUR** normal.

This spring break offered us a chance to achieve a sense of our own self defined "normalcy" as we booked a last minute trip to Las Vegas. On March 12th we consulted with Marnie's oncologist, and he gave us the "green light" to travel. In true Foreman fashion we scoured the Internet to find a financially friendly deal that met our weather and entertainment needs. Vegas it was!

On March 22nd we headed to Grand Forks, North Dakota and jumped on Allegiant Air to reach our destination. This in itself was a bit of a culture shock and was definitely not the pampering we normally receive from our status with Air Canada. I had to chuckle when both kids displayed their disappointment that we would not be going to the "Maple Leaf" Lounge for refreshments prior to departure. This was only forgotten and forgiven when they realized that the aircraft did not have TV's! How did the plane ever manage to leave the ground??? Our poor children...

Vegas was great. We toured Hoover Dam, Red Rocks Canyon (a must see if you are going to Vegas), and every factory shopping outlet known to mankind! We even managed to see a couple of shows. We were marvelled by the performance of Le Reve, and equally impressed with the magic of Criss Angel. Although tired, and fighting a bad cold, Marnie kept up, and outpaced us all. What a treat to get side tracked by the distractions of Las Vegas. Who knew we would consider this place our "normal"?

On Tuesday of this week we were welcomed back to reality as we once again visited the Victoria Hospital for pre-chemotherapy blood work. All tests were within normal range and we were given the go ahead for our next round. Marnie was also thoroughly checked out to see if she has a respiratory infection. Dr. Ogaranko felt that her cold is viral but for precautionary reasons prescribed a course of antibiotics. This will help in case her existing cold develops into something more as her immune system weakens with chemo.

On Wednesday we started our third session of therapy and were once again welcomed by the smiling faces of our nurses, Delleen, and Colette. Consistency is key as you go through this process and our nurse team is getting to know Marnie quite well and has developed a very trusting bond with her. This has been a godsend. Wednesday evening saw Marnie attend a much needed "Stitch Club" meeting with some of her girlfriends. Not quite sure what goes on at these clandestine gatherings (very top secret), but appreciate the mental vacation and many laughs that this provides for her.

The remainder of the week has been very good as Marnie's mom and dad came in to Winnipeg for a visit and to give her some extra TLC. Marnie continues to marvel us all with her determination and strength. Thanks again for all the e-mails, cards, and demonstrations of love and support. Team Marnie rocks!

Until the next update.....Brian, Marnie, Madison, and Brayden...

April 25th, 2013

Hello Team Marnie,

Well, another three weeks has passed since we updated "our team" on Marnie's Journey. These weeks have been filled with many accomplishments that leave us proud and optimistic about the future.

Marnie has fought off her bad cold, and although it is still lingering a bit, was once again cleared for her final chemo treatment of round one. This was completed on Tuesday morning. We are grateful for her fabulous team at the Victoria Hospital (Kristin, Delleen, and Claudette). Thanks again for empathy, your TLC, and your smiles; you made a frightening situation, bearable. We don't know how you do it, but are very thankful that you do!

"It is often in the darkest skies that
we see the brightest stars."

RICHARD EVANS

The next steps for Marnie include managing the side effects of this last infusion, and then another CT scan scheduled on May 14th to assess the progress of treatment thus far. We will wait patiently for these results as we do not see Dr. Pitz (our oncologist) until May 28th. This will be a very nerve racking time for us, but we are full of hope that Marnie is fighting a winning battle!

This is not the only accomplishment that has happened in our household recently. We are proud of Madison for passing her written driver's test and obtaining her learner's permit. She is a little nervous behind the wheel, but getting more confident every day. At our Twins Hockey banquet last week Brayden received his team's award for "The Hardest Working Player". No doubt this is a trait that comes from his mother. For those of you who have competed with, and or against Marnie, or have witnessed her fight this disease, you will understand what I am talking about.

We would also like to express our gratitude to the Twins organization, and its families for allowing our Minor Peewee team to hold a live auction for Cancer Care at the banquet. This was a continuation to the "Buzzing it off for Marnie" fundraising campaign. The money made here, plus the initial fundraising from

Bruce M's "haircut", have raised in excess of $15,000. Special acknowledgement to John L., Mark E., Tim C., The Winnipeg Jets, The Winnipeg Blues Bombers, and Malach Company for your generous prize donations. Shout outs to Bruce M. for your coordination and passion towards making this happen, and to Gord J. and Paolo S. for your auctioneering talents!

Once again thanks for all your messages of support, your meals, your thoughts and prayers. We communicated earlier this week to many of my Pfizer colleagues that current events around us leave us to question the good in others, but the one thing that astounds us is the quality of people, "our team", that we have around us. We are continually blown away by the random acts of kindness that are displayed by our friends and family and our community. We love you all, and are so appreciative to have you in our lives.

Until our much anticipated next update on May 28th…

Brian, Marnie, Madison, and Brayden

TIME OUT

*"The moment you doubt whether you can fly,
you cease for ever to be able to do it."*

PETER PAN — J.M. BARRIE.

RECAP

At this point on the path of our cancer journey, we were immersed in process, system, and schedule. There seemed little time to get stuck in any kind of negatives because, just as we would head toward a pothole, kindness would cushion the bump. A positive message would arrive via email, Facebook, or in person. Sure, there were moments when fear reared its scary head, but we discovered courage in ourselves that we never knew existed.

COACH'S CORNER

What we did to help ourselves.

We took the attitude of preparing for the worst while hoping for the best. Shortly after Marnie's first chemo treatment she quickly re-gained her strength and, on a whim, we decided to take a family vacation to Las Vegas. These dates corresponded with spring break. We were desperate to escape the news of our diagnosis and have some family fun. Where else but Vegas?

We had a great time enjoying the sights in and around Las Vegas. We emphasize, regardless of your budget, it is great to escape for a bit, even if it's somewhere local.

As the week went on, Marnie developed a nasty cold accompanied by wicked coughing fits. We monitored her symptoms to ensure she was not spiking a fever as a sign of infection. She worried about the noise she was making and we found her several times, throughout the week, sleeping on the bathroom floor or in the bathtub, so as to not interrupt our sleep. This was Marnie.

Hindsight is 20/20. We learned a lot from the Vegas adventure. Use Boy Scout lore and 'Always Be Prepared!' From that time on, we never left the house, whether a weekend getaway or family trip, without our medical bag. We always carried a broad spectrum antibiotic, cough suppressants, laxatives, and anti-diarrhea options, pain/fever pills, and anti-nausea medications. Everything at our fingertips in case we needed pharmaceutical help. We recommend speaking to your doctor or oncologist and putting together such a pack. Interestingly, we never had to access this kit on any other family endeavors.

BRIAN: Las Vegas did provide an excellent distraction for Madison and Brayden. Walking the strip certainly provided life education. Never have they stayed so close to Mom and Dad! As a mobile billboard stopped in front of us while we were waiting to cross the street, eleven year old Brayden turned to us and said, "Why would I want a college girl delivered to my door?" We laughed and then hesitated before replying, "tutoring!" He accepted our answer and moved on to the next distraction. Vegas through the eyes of a pre-teen: priceless!

What else?

We wanted to learn more about supplements and superfoods—needing to create the least hospitable environment for the cancer, cope with the chemotherapy, and create the healthiest conditions for Marnie by boosting her immune system. In essence our goal was strengthening the immune system to aid in the killing of cancer.

Before you try herbals or supplements check with your doctor or cancer pharmacist. You will receive a lot of thoughtful advice about the 'extras' you should be taking as adjunctive therapy with your chemotherapy. Everyone has a relative or friend that tried something outside of their treatment regimen that helped them with their own personal journey. We were no exception.

On top of Marnie's prescribed therapies, we consulted with a natural health practitioner, in Vancouver, who gave us some evidence-based advice on what we needed to change in order to try and reverse the cancer path.

We want to make it very clear that, before we tried any of these holistic options, we consulted our oncologist and a CancerCare Manitoba assigned pharmacist.

Vitamin C, Turkey Tail, Urea, Essiac Tea, AHCC, MGN3, Vitamin D, Curcumin, and GCMAF were all added to our armamentarium in hopes of beating the disease. We learned the importance of reducing sugar intake, eating properly with more organic fruits and vegetable, while reducing our animal proteins and fats.

We studied hydration and pure, clean water and its impact on therapy.

And we opened up our world to the science of juicing. Ah yes, juicing… spending hours on the internet finding the perfect recipes that would help to cleanse the liver while boosting the immune system.

Once the research was done, it was time to purchase the perfect juicer. And, where else would we find this other than Kijiji? After many calls, we decided to purchase a juicer from a lady named Tanya, in the nearby community of Bridgewater.

Right from the greeting at her front door, Tanya struck up a friendly conversation. An avid gardener, with two small children, she'd purchased the appliance to help out a friend who was going through his or her own cancer journey. When she found out the synergy in our reasons, she handed over the juicer, wished us the best of luck, and refused to take payment.

Random acts of kindness show up in many ways from many different sources. We were able to see the good in so many from such a bad life experience. We returned later that day with some lilies for her to plant in her garden. Hopefully these will appear annually and serve as a reminder of her thoughtfulness and generosity.

Juicing itself was an interesting experience. Beets, carrots, apples, oranges, lemons, limes, ginger, cinnamon, parsley, spinach, kale, and wheat grass were combined in various fashions to make an 'untasty treat' for Marnie.

We tried like heck to create the perfect juice; one with the essential ingredients that was actually palatable. This was not to happen. No matter how bad the juice tasted, Marnie consumed it, twice a day. The thought of the benefit far outweighed the horrible taste. She would have done anything to be cured of cancer.

What others did that was helpful.

They showed up on our doorstep with blankets: handmade woven afghans, fleece covers and, incredibly, an original quilt created for us, courtesy of the Stitch group. We used these blankets to curl up in and watch our favorite TV shows, or to wrap around us when we read a good book or magazine. These items were a constant reminder of the love and support we were continually receiving.

The amount of goodness that came our way was simply overwhelming. It is accurate to say that 'thoughtfulness' itself is healing. Love, laughter, and compassion are truly the best medicine.

Fundraising. Awareness led to fundraising for various aspects of cancer research and living with cancer. Not directly to us, but for all. That's what other people did; they demonstrated support for us by helping everyone touched by cancer. The haircuts—buzz cuts—supported Marnie in terms of honouring her and recognizing her situation, and the funds raised had a ripple effect and benefitted others. These kinds of activities created and originated by one or more friends grew into huge events, the results of which are still ongoing and will benefit people we've never met and likely never will.

What the professionals did.

Again, providing the backup, notes, and diagrams helped a great deal as we moved to further stages of treatment. For example: explaining the facts about HER2-positive—but not as if we were medical students. Thorough, simple, not candy-coated: HER2-positive (which Marnie did not have) is a breast cancer test that tests positive for a protein called human epidermal growth factor receptor 2. One out of every five breast cancers exhibit this gene mutation that makes an excess of HER2 protein. So what did they do? They helped up prepare for the worst while hoping for the best. And they did this with an unparalleled brand of professionalism and caring.

Humour. The professionals were not just all about the facts, but demonstrated— numerous times—they were real. They shed a tear, I'm sure, and they rallied, and they told great jokes, and found humour in many aspects of their work. Their ability to 'serve' showed through in every part of their duties—so much so, duty did not enter into the picture, or job description—they were comedians with wings, caregivers with wide shoulders; they wore their hearts on their sleeves.

JUNIOR LEAGUE: MADISON

No matter how Mom was feeling, she would always drive out to Morden, Winkler, Altona, Morris — anywhere, really - to watch me play soccer. She was always the loudest Mom (positive and negative) at sporting events.

THREE STARS

- Remember that the professionals are human beings, too. Just because they don't sugar coat the facts doesn't mean they're not devastated you have the disease.
- No matter how exhausted you become: file, note-take, organize, sort, write down questions when you think of them.
- By all means, thank your team, but do not feel guilty over what members of your team are doing for you, or what they are 'starting' (in terms of spearheading fundraisers). This is their journey—they have a route too.

OVERTIME

On Juicing

http://www.mayoclinic.org/healthy-lifestyle/nutrition-and-healthy-eating/ expert-blog/safe-juicing/bgp-20056204

On sorting out the roles dietician/nutritionist/qualifications

https://myvega.com/blog/registered-dietician-vs-nutritionist/

On humour

http://www.mayoclinic.org/healthy-lifestyle/stress-management/ in-depth/stress-relief/art-20044456

PLAYER PROFILE

(taken directly and chronologically from the eulogy and shared over the chapters of this book)

"She loved to Travel!

We were fortunate to see many parts of the world together. Corpus Christie, Los Angeles, Las Vegas, San Francisco, Orlando, Anna Maria Island, San Antonio, Boston, New York, Vancouver, Calgary, Toronto, Hawaii, Stockholm, Helsinki, Copenhagen, Tallin, St. Petersburg, Rome, Cuba, Cancun, Freeport, Nassau, and the Exumas to name many. We created countless memories together on these adventures. She was great to travel with.

Marnie was a planner. We knew what we were doing and when we were going to do it before we got there. Maps were obtained, destinations were highlighted and itineraries were followed. She did not want to miss a thing. She immersed herself in each community and culture that we visited, respecting their ways and learning about their history.

She would spend time talking to the locals and hours reading the coffee table books that were provided in the hotel rooms to find out more about where we were, the people that were there, and additional interesting venues to see.

We followed her through shops, churches, museums, restaurants and many local attractions. When we were in Rome, we were visiting the Vatican museum. It was a long tour, full of thousands upon thousands of tapestries, maps, and artifacts. It was a long day and each room was starting to look like the next. While I saw yet another item hanging on the wall, Marnie took the time to learn more about who made it, the era it came from, and its significance. While I passed by an urn sitting on the table, she wanted to know why it was there, why it was significant, and what its story was. I soon realized how refreshing this was. (She made these moments learning experiences for me.) I started to see the world through her eyes, (and I appreciated we could) learn together.

Churches and Museums became less of a chore and more of a learning experience. It was the teacher in her.

I mentioned the destinations we travelled to, but these were very secondary to Marnie. It wasn't about the location. It was about spending time with her family, and her friends, away from our normal busy lives.

She carried this theme into our home. Marnie loved company. Whether you were staying over for the weekend, or over for dinner, the moment you came through the doors you were family. She wanted to know all about you, your family, how your week was, and your stories. We would spend hours at our dining room table or kitchen island with many of you, over a glass of wine, learning about your successes, your failures, and basically becoming better friends. She was a catalyst for this.

She was also not afraid to let you know when you had worn out your welcome and identify when it was time to leave. There was a time when we were living on Burlington Way when we had an unexpected late night visit from Marnie's cousins, Martin and Brock, and her father, Brian. They may or may not have already had a few sodas, and rumor has it that they may have been looking for a couple more. They were not really adhering to a low level of volume at this time either. Marnie had had enough. You could hear the footsteps from upstairs and see the image of Marnie coming through the family room. She pointed to Martin, Brock, and her father, and calmly said, you, you, and you, get the "bleep" out of my house. Not many words were spoken. They got up and left. They knew better than to mess with that fiery redhead that evening. It is a story we still laugh about when we get together."

Six

PLAY BY PLAY

May 28, 2013

Hello Team Marnie,

On April 23rd Marnie completed her **first cycle of four rounds** of chemotherapy treatment. She once again handled the treatment and post chemo side effects very well. Although she experienced periods of fatigue, these were far fewer than the previous three rounds. As being less tired was a bonus, other adverse events began to settle in. Numbness/tingling in her fingers and toes presented, and still exists today. She is also starting to show signs of losing some fingernails. All are common experiences with Taxotere.

Throughout this, spring hockey has been in full force, and Marnie was able to accompany our Junior Bison team to several weekend hockey tournaments. These trips are excellent distractions as both the hockey and shopping provide a much needed mental holiday from the daily reminders of living with cancer. It was great to see our camping neighbours and friends as we attended the Stars and Stripes tournament in Minneapolis.

May 13th was a special time in our house this year. Not only for the obvious reasons, but it uncovered a hidden talent of our daughter, Madison. For many years she stepped away from taking art at school. This year she

---

changed, and has definitely found a calling. She painted her mom a picture and presented it to her on Mother's Day! Very special indeed.

May 14th Marnie returned to the St. Boniface Hospital for a CT scan to monitor the progress of her chemotherapy. The results of these tests would be delivered to us on May 28th (today). To say these last two weeks have tested our patience while we wait for the results would be an understatement. During this kind of stress, one can experience emotional highs and lows, and bouts of 'startling awake' in the middle of the night, hoping and praying that treatment is working.

We are thankful for our busy calendar, full of kids' activities, and the constant encouragement from our friends. We keep a binder in our family room that contains every e-mail that you've sent. Marnie reads these often. These keep us in a positive mindset and channel our energy to where it needs to be; helping her get better.

May 28th, today, we visited CancerCare for our appointment with Dr. Pitz and to get our much anticipated results.

The theme of the day is definitely "cautious optimism". The chest CT scan demonstrated that the Lymph node tumours have all reduced in size and are now under a centimetre. The spots within her breast are also smaller. The abdominal CT scan showed no change in the liver tumour sizes, but also showed no new nodules.

Dr. Pitz is very positive with this news, and this is proof that Marnie is "Fighting Like a Girl".

Next steps...Marnie will start the **second cycle—round one of four** of chemotherapy tomorrow morning at the Victoria Hospital. We will continue on with the Taxotere treatment and will monitor side effects closely. If the tingling in her fingers and toes gets worse they will stop treatment so as not to cause permanent damage to these extremities. We are hoping that we can get in another 4 rounds, (each cycle = four rounds followed by a CT scan) but realize that we may have to stop because of this. Once she completes this cycle, she will be put on an anti-oestrogen therapy called Tamoxifen which reduces or stops cancer growth all together.

On June 16th, look out for Team Marnie at the Manitoba Marathon as Brent F, Kevin S, Mike A, Troy H, and I set out as a relay team in support of Marnie. Like Cancer therapy, slow and steady wins the race!

We know this may seem like a broken record, but we thank all of you for your continued love, support, and prayers. We truly believe that you are all making a difference in how Marnie is battling this disease. Together we can do this.

Until our next update…

Brian, Marnie, Madison, and Brayden

TIME OUT

"A shaft of sunlight at the end of a dark afternoon, a note of music, and the way the back of a baby's neck smells if its mother keeps it tidy," answered Henry. "Correct," said Stuart. "Those are the important things. You forgot one thing, though. Mary Bendix, what did Henry Rackmeyer forget?" "He forgot ice cream with chocolate sauce on it," said Mary quickly."

STUART LITTLE. — E. B. WHITE.

RECAP

Milestones. Many of us measure our calendar lives by events (Mother's Day, Birthdays, Graduations, Independence Day, Canada Day, Ramadan, Yom Kippur; you get the idea.) In a cancer journey, the calendar plays a key role and thoughts can drift to what ifs. At this point we were nearing the six month mark—a milestone of sorts: half a year.

The mind can go to strange places during a battle: thoughts of what if this had 'just' been breast cancer? (Imagine hoping for that?) Projections of where we might have been had the original diagnosis remained as such. Visions of what life would be in a cancer free post-double-mastectomy world. Apparently those strange places are not that strange; quite normal in fact. Take a little fatigue, a measure of time, a dash of frustration, some eye of bat, and *SHIZZAM,* you've created 'the best place NOT to go'. But it's okay if you catch yourself there. Just come back to reality. And take one more step forward.

And when you return—oh, yes!—nothing says welcome back like ice cream and chocolate sauce.

It's important to have favourites or versions of favourites. Labeling everything that goes into your mouth as good and bad doesn't do anything for a healthy mindset. Yet it's important to be conscious—to have a healthy awareness—of how chemicals react in the body. That goes for the stuff we refer to as food and the stuff we refer to as medicine, for it is all chemical. As far as emotional therapy, the little mouse was right (let's not forget he had a brilliant narrator in E.B. White): there's nothing like a shaft of sunlight at the end of a dark day. We had many of each, and we moved through the lows and clung to the light.

Mother's Day. The gift from Madison exampled how things can change. From not taking art to taking it; the painting Madison produced reminded us of choice—had she not chosen to give art a chance? We drew from this and chose to move forward.

COACH'S CORNER

What we did to help ourselves.

As much as one does not want to celebrate chemotherapy, there were milestones. We'd reached a certain amount of therapy—who would think someone would want to celebrate the body's ability to handle toxins.

As well, having reminders of progress and hope were important. Printing and filing replies to our emails was energy-giving; reading them, therapeutic. The binder filled with replies could be likened to that sliver of light so needed at the end of the day.

We think it would be a great idea for those without a large support system to have a regular supply of motivational books and movies, and interesting autobiographies of much admired heroes.

We dealt with side effects—meaning Marnie dealt with side-effects, and we dealt with Marnie dealing with side-effects. There were many mornings when Marnie woke with the feelings of pins and needles in her feet. We've all experienced this sensation when we've slept in a funny position—when an arm or foot feels like it is falling asleep—but this was constant; some days were worse than others. Continuous foot rubs and walking helped to ease the sensation and/or take attention from the condition. It is strange what a person begins to get used to or learns to live with when there is a much bigger prize in mind—that being survival. Lesson being: don't sweat the small stuff.

What others did that was helpful.

Five months in and all systems—friends and connections—were go, go, go.

Support flowed in. Uplifting messages and practical actions continued, and we accepted them all with gratitude. Meals continued to be organized, rides appeared, and the crew behind the scenes directed and produced palpable results in the 'positive thinking department'. We were urged on by the gestures of others.

Whether in groups or independently, people continued to help.

If you are a friend of someone who has cancer, don't ever discount a small gesture thinking it might not be enough, isn't much, or won't make a difference. No act of kindness is too small.

> *BRIAN: Chemo day was always stressful. And every treatment day a care package arrived on our front step—delivered by our good friend, Jane. It usually contained a trashy magazine, a vitamin water, and a thoughtfully chosen card. This gesture meant the world to Marnie.*
>
> *When someone did something thoughtful, Marnie knew that those kind-hearted friends were with her in spirit. In this case, she pictured Jane's friendship as she faced another infusion.*
>
> *Visits, from others, when she was at the hospital for treatments, were uplifting. Friendly faces in a 'not so friendly place, because of a not so friendly disease' brightened Marnie's day. Often, those smiling folks came with a bonus of a Tim Horton's coffee, and transformed Marnie's world in the moment.*
>
> *These gestures were not only appreciated by Marnie, but buoyed me. Sharing through thoughtful acts of kindness eased the burden of all that was happening to our family. We each felt the love from the smallest gestures.*

What the professionals did.

Medicine can seem like magic, and those who perform surgery, diagnose illness, or perform tests, appear as magicians.

The professionals reminded us how easy it is to cross the line when dealing with incoming information. We were advised not to overload ourselves by micromanaging and over-studying. Where we'd once delved into every aspect of the disease, we now became selective about what to study and when. We did not want to get 'medical student syndrome'.

It's a fine line doctors must walk to explain drug choices and side effects to patients, especially ones as curious as us; and, as a patient, how much information to collect. Some would say 'collect all the information' but, just like the medical student who—when learning about various diseases—begins to believe he displays the symptoms of the 'disease of that week's homework', there can be an overload and some transference.

Such is the case with side effects. Go onto any website and input any drug's name and you'll get the compulsory liability list. Go a little deeper and the next thing that happens—since you know you have the disease—you believe you have the side effects. The mind is a powerful computer. Choice is an excellent software package that operates in the brain. Exercising choice and implementing a balanced approach to information is paramount.

Take, for example, Marnie's side effects—numbness—from the Taxotere. The tingling and numbness was real. Our doctor had explained that she might experience these, but did not go into detail in terms of every rarely reported side effect that would appear on laboratory documentation for 'liability' purposes.

We appreciated the professionals in our lives reminding us of that balance.

THREE STARS

- Sleep is underrated. It's the time when we heal mentally and physically. Make sure all household members are getting their z's.
- Motivational materials are essential to moving forward.

- Celebrate everything. Treasure every event not related to cancer. Rejoice at every intersection of triumph over cancer. Pain free for an hour? Yahoo it up.

JUNIOR LEAGUE: BRAYDEN

I always loved to go to Jets games with Mom. She always had fun at the games. She'd cheer loud and often. I liked going because, the thing is, I could talk to her about anything and she would pretend to care, even though I knew she didn't. I mean, she cared, I know she cared about me, but some of what I went on about was a bit lame, and because she loved me she just acted like it was the most important stuff in the world, because she knew it was important to me.

OVERTIME

https://hbr.org/2011/05/the-power-of-small-wins

https://www.caregiver.org/taking-care-you-self-care-family-caregivers

PLAYER PROFILE

(taken directly and chronologically from the eulogy and shared over the chapters of this book)

"Marnie was a reality TV junkie…She never missed an episode of Survivor, The Amazing Race, Master Chef, The Biggest Loser, The Bachelor, or the Bachelorette.

Our family would have pools and all throw in a few dollars and bet on who would win Survivor. I would drive her crazy when I would make fun of the contestants on the Bachelor. "Hard to believe that 25 women living in a house together all trying to date and marry one man have never been in a stable relationship and are unable to find love?" Who knew?

The one reality station that cost me a lot of money is HGTV or Home and Garden Television. I was quite happy with our outdated kitchen and worn down bathrooms. I would argue with Marnie that our house was fine. Would the food taste any different? Would a new shower get me any cleaner? Well apparently the answer was yes, as over the past three years all three have been renovated. Once again, not a time to cross the redhead."

Seven

PLAY BY PLAY

July 11, 2013

Hello Team Marnie,

Hope you and your families are all having a wonderful summer.

I've been getting a lot of texts and e-mails asking about Marnie's journey, so wanted to provide a quick update on her progress.

Yesterday was a bit of a milestone as Marnie completed round seven of her Taxotere (chemo) treatment.

As we mentioned in our earlier communication, most patients (and we know Marnie is not most patients) are able to handle around six treatments due to the side effects of tingling sensations in toes and fingers. This has to be closely monitored as if it gets out of control it can cause permanent nerve damage and loss of feeling. Although she has been experiencing this, it has not progressed to the point of discontinuing therapy.

We will continue to watch for this and hope we can get our last treatment in on August 7th (which also happens to be our 20th wedding anniversary!).

Marnie continues to do amazingly. We have been able to do weekend visits to friends' cabins, attend many of our kids sporting events, and are looking forward to getting away for some summer camping.

August will once again be a month of angst as on August 13th we go for another CT scan to monitor treatment progress. We then will visit our oncologist Dr. Pitz on the 20th to get our results and determine our path forward.

Please keep your fingers and toes crossed for positive results.

Father's Day was a big day for Team Marnie, as the "Fight Like a Girl" relay team (Brent F. Troy H., Kevin S., Mike A., and I) competed in the Manitoba Marathon.

We are happy to report that all finished with no injury and achieved a time of 3:18:58. This was good enough for 18th place with over 650 teams competing! Still think they should go by weight class and not time. Would have been a first place finish for sure...

Nice to see friends and family cheering us on along the way.

Thanks to all of you once again for the many gestures of support, the texts, e-mails, phone calls, and visits. They mean so much to us and continue to demonstrate that we are not alone in this fight.

Have a great summer everyone!

Until our next update…

Brian, Marnie, Madison, and Brayden

August 20, 2013

Hello Team Marnie,

It is very hard to believe we are approaching the end of August and that we have been on this trek for almost nine months now. Thank goodness for the many distractions along the way, and this summer has been no different. For those that thought that cancer would slow us down they could not be more wrong.

July saw us take a weekend trip to Minneapolis for a soccer tournament and then we were off to Oak Lake Beach (near Virden) to be with our good friends Connie and Kirby, and Darren and Trudy from British Columbia. It was great to see them and their families and have a chance to re-connect. It really does feel like time has stood still when we get together.

After coming back to Winnipeg, we once again ventured down the Trans-Canada Highway to Saskatchewan. I was scheduled to do some work there, so the whole family piled in the car and we ventured to Regina, Saskatoon, and then spent a wonderful weekend in Waskesiu to officially start our vacation. It was great to stop off in Hamiota on the way home to spend time with family. Thanks to the Brooks and Hawkins brood for your hospitality!

Our first week of vacation was getting prepared for our annual camping trip to Bemidji, Minnesota, and visiting with friends. It was wonderful to spend an evening with Kevin, Jen, and Jack who visited us from California. Thanks for taking the time to include us in your hectic schedule.

Week two had us venture to Bemidji. This is always a highlight of our year. We were joined this summer by the Male (in their 28 foot RV – a sight to see), and Bryant families who both experienced Cass Lake for the first time.

Although the weather was not that warm, there were plenty of activities to keep us on the go. As always, it was great to see the Gerritsen and Thompson families. We have been camping with them for almost 10 years. Cass Lake would not be the same without them.

Our vacation was not without sadness as we were alerted on August 2nd that Marnie's uncle, Cam Brown, had passed away. He was a great man; loved and respected by all that met him. We will miss him dearly.

On August 7th, our 20th Wedding anniversary, Marnie completed round eight of chemotherapy. She has been feeling very good this past week (despite the ever present tingling in her toes and fingers from treatment). She helped us run our Annual Winnipeg Blues Alumni Golf Tournament, attended a Blue Bomber game (thanks Dale D.), and even managed a great day at Grand Beach and Lockport on the Saturday. Marnie also completed her CT scan on August 13th.

Thanks to longtime friend Ed B. from Dallas who managed to squeeze a visit in on travels through Manitoba.

So, this brings us to today. We once again come back to Hope and Optimism. I think back to January and the emotions that consumed us. The many tears, the sleepless nights, and all of the uncertainty. Today was a little different. Today, both of us shared some tears of joy. It appears that the chemotherapy is working, and working well.

I will cite the report that was given to us today, and is in comparison to the scan that was completed in May.

"There has been a significant decrease in the size of the majority of the liver lesions. For example a lesion within the right lobe of the dome has decreased in size from 8 mm to 5 mm. In addition, there was a lesion within the lateral segment of the hepatic lobe inferiorly that is no longer visualized.

No new hepatic lesions are demonstrated...There has been improvement in the multiple hepatic lesions".

This was combined with Dr. Pitz telling us that all lymph nodes are back to normal size and that the breast has been stabilized (it may actually be smaller- but not worthy of comment on the CT). All news is extremely positive. Marnie is truly "fighting like a girl"!

What does all this mean? It means that we continue with treatment. Dr. Pitz said it is "uncommon" and "rare" that an individual can handle more than eight rounds of treatment (insert "STUBBORN" here). He is incredibly impressed with the determination and positive spirit that Marnie has displayed and has recommended another four rounds of Taxotere. He believes in treating as aggressively as possible, and with the results that have been achieved, we should not stop. We agree.

On August 28th, we will start round nine (with hope of getting to twelve).

Constant monitoring of the tingling sensation will have to be done as to whether we can continue. Our nurse says that constant "foot rubs" can help with this sensation. Any volunteers?

Until our next update ...

Brian, Marnie, Madison, and Brayden

December 2, 2013

Hello Team Marnie,

We hope that this e-mail finds you all in good health as we approach the holiday season.

Our last update was in August. After our busy summer, we thought we would ease back into our normal routines as school commenced. Once again, we were mistaken.

September saw Madison finishing her Community soccer playoffs with Whyte Ridge, while starting her fall soccer and volleyball seasons with Sanford High School.

Brayden was, once again, at the rink trying out (and making) the Twins AA Hockey team. In between these activities, Marnie and I managed to sneak off for a 5 day weekend to Las Vegas with friends. It was a wonderful trip, filled with great food, fellowship, and much needed laughter. Thanks to Connie and Kirby, and Scott and Karen who made the trip from Vancouver and Calgary respectively, and to Mark, Sharon, Kevin, and Tracey who we joined from Winnipeg. Saw some things I will remember for life, and a few things I am having a hard time forgetting…

In October/November we were off to celebrate our 20th wedding anniversary, we packed our bags and headed on vacation.

One of Marnie's items on her "bucket list" was to stay in a bungalow over the ocean. After much research, the island of Tahiti offered this option. Although it took a while to get there, it was well worth it. This was the perfect balance of activities and relaxation. The resort offered a great beach/pool area where we could hang out, snorkel, kayak, or go for a swim. The island allowed us to do much sightseeing including swimming with sharks, and sting rays, and a jungle safari where we viewed the amazing waterfalls and vegetation in the area. We were thrilled to be joined by Mark and Sharon E. on this adventure. Thank you for your patience and sense of adventure. You helped make this an amazing experience.

During all of this, Marnie was receiving rounds 9-12 of chemotherapy. She once again handled all of this with amazing courage and grace.

Round 9 saw her experience similar side effects to her previous treatments (finger and toe numbness, and joint pain), but rounds 10-12 added in a new twist, that being edema. This is a very common side effect of Taxotere and is defined as fluid retention in the body. Marnie's edema was most prominent in her legs and feet, but also presented in her arms, wrists and fingers. Although she received a diuretic (Lasix - a powerful water pill) to help alleviate this side effect, the flare ups caused much leg heaviness and discomfort. It seems to be getting better each day.

I mentioned at the beginning of our journey that Marnie was a strong, somewhat, stubborn person. Well she definitely proved this true. To put things into perspective, most patients are not able to go past round eight on full dose Taxotere. Her Twelve rounds at full dose are nothing short of amazing to me and to her doctors.

I laugh when we visit Dr. Ogaranko (G.P. oncologist) and he asks how Marnie is feeling, and she responds "I was only able to curl three times this week". She really is mad about this, because she missed that 4th game!

This defines her, and demonstrates the spirit she has displayed for the past 11 months.

Alright...so let's talk about today, and the results that we received from her CT scan. When Dr. Pitz walked into the office he asked if anyone had spoken to us about our results, and after a period of silence, he uttered, "the scans were great"… "the cancer continues to recede and is getting smaller".

The report from radiology states: "There has been a significant improvement in the metastatic liver disease and most of the lesions have virtually disappeared. There are still three tiny nodules that exist in the liver, but no new lesions have been identified". IMPRESSION...the liver metastatic disease has significantly improved, with a few remaining lesions still identified. What a fabulous early Christmas present!

So what does this mean? From what we have learned today, the cancer still exists in Marnie's body, but appears to be under control.

As in previous communications, her cancer is incurable but treatable. The doctors feel that Marnie has had a maximum response to Taxotere treatment and would like to give her a body a break and step down her treatment to Tamoxifen.

The goal now is to keep the disease under control, while minimizing side effects, and improve her quality of life. She will continue to have CT scans and oncology visits every 3 months to monitor disease progression/regression. We will also be visiting a surgeon on December 12th to explore more options.

Guardian Angels - angels believed to have special care of a particular individual; people who look after or are concerned with the welfare of others.

In October Marnie and I were exposed to a very unique fundraiser as we attended the 22nd annual benefit for Women's Cancer. It is here that we watched many cancer patients and survivor's proudly "strut their stuff" during a fashion show to a sold out audience at the Winnipeg Convention Centre. They have all been through so much; each with a unique story. These "models for a day" were appropriately named "Angels". They, like us, have garnished their strength from their families, friends, and communities.

We have learned so much along the way about cancer, its diagnosis, and treatment but perhaps our biggest life lesson through all of this is that there are so many caring people out there. We are fortunate to have had many of you help us out along the way, and again want to thank all of you; our Guardian Angels.

Until our next update ...

Brian, Marnie, Madison, and Brayden

TIME OUT

*"What is done cannot be undone, but one
can prevent it happening again."*
*"I don't think of all the misery but of
the beauty that still remains."*
"Whoever is happy will make others happy too."

The Diary of a Young Girl — Anne Frank.

RECAP

In most ways we were no different than other families, we had commitments that included regular medical appointments for each member; dentist appointments and checkups. Parent/teacher interviews came up just like they do in any parent's life, and outside our involvement with sports there was just the act of simply vegging and watching television. On top of this was the entire realm of cancer-journey related appointments, reading, research, and documentation.

COACH'S CORNER

What we did to help ourselves.

We had a party! A post Taxotere party! A Cancer is under control Party! We opened up our house to all who had helped and supported us through this phase. We told stories, we laughed, we hugged, we smiled, and we turned back the clock to a time that cancer did not exist. It was an amazing night.

BRIAN: I remember sitting in our family room, looking through to our kitchen, and seeing Marnie. She was beaming as she was surrounded by the comfort of our friends. No needles, no nurses, no doctors, just a steady infusion of love from those who mattered.

We travelled. We were not afraid: if we could have cancer at home, then we could have cancer on the road. Marnie made it easy by continuing to blend positivity with the strength of her stubbornness and, because of that, we celebrated nature, rejoiced with friends, and opened ourselves to adventure.

We intended to cross things off our bucket list. 2013 was the year of our 20th wedding anniversary. The date, August 7th, corresponded with one of our chemo treatments.

BRIAN: I woke up early and snuck out to buy flowers and chocolates then took them to the Victoria Hospital and hid them by Marnie's regular treatment chair and closed the privacy curtain.

When we arrived, she was rather perturbed that someone had taken her usual spot. "Of all the days this had to happen".

We opened the curtain to display the floral arrangement and treats. A smile came across her face. "This was not the place I had in mind to celebrate our 20th anniversary!"

As we sat down I opened my laptop to a prepared presentation. A surprise two-week trip to Tahiti, where we would stay in a 'hut' over the ocean; a place we'd dreamed of going.

We shared this journey with two special friends. The travel was long, but well worth it. We enjoyed the sunsets, swam with the sharks, took tours of the jungle, and waded in the streams and pools created by mountain waterfalls. It was an incredible experience.

You may have read my mind; I'm guessing I could read yours if you took your loved one to a spiritual or wondrous place. So, yes, (of course) I hoped and prayed that somehow the pristine water had some miraculous healing power and had created a cure for Marnie's condition.

Outside of our travels and the celebration: we reminded ourselves of the importance of sleep, and though it seemed like we were everywhere with everyone, we did say no to some things. Somehow, probably through Marnie's incredible drive, we moved forward, and the basic items were checked off our lists, and some fun ones were added and checked off too.

In hindsight, we'd advise each individual not to feel he or she has to measure up to the heroic stories of others, but to be the best 'self' possible.

And to stretch a little in terms of learning more and experiencing more—spiritual, mental, and physical growth often occurs outside one's comfort zone. Stretch, but be gentle with yourself. No one is (or need be) a specialist in every department; even superheroes have their limits. You need only be an informed and proactive version of you. You're doing the best you can with the skills you have in each moment.

What others did that was helpful.

They travelled with us. Physically, as in the two friends who accompanied us, but in all other forms—caring for the children in our absence, sending emails, cooking food, fundraising for ALL those involved with cancer. If anything shifted—at this nine month mark—it was that, though it seemed impossible, there was even more caring, deeper love, and closer relationships.

Nature helped us, and I would advise that wherever your location, get that feeling of the earth under your feet. Notice nature even in the tiniest places:

grass forcing its way through the concrete sidewalk; moss growing on a building; the life cycle of leaves. Focus on small wonders that make up the larger picture.

Fundraising. Again, this was a way we could share the kindness of our support system with others. People were so good to us; in for a penny in for a pound with relays, and potlucks, and whatever struck their fancy. I was told that it helped others feel that they were helping heal Marnie. It also put them in touch with new friends and associations that they'd never have met if it were not for our journey. When funds were raised for the good of all, we were elated.

BRIAN: A good friend of mine who is a local Winnipeg radio personality had lost his wife Alanna to breast cancer in March 2011. Joe is one of the most philanthropic people in Winnipeg, giving his time generously.

He will help anyone with a good cause. His dedication to volunteerism is inspiring. With his wife's passing, Joe dedicated his time to raising funds for Palliative Care in Manitoba by lending his name to a charity golf tournament.

Marnie loved to golf! We first played in this tournament in 2012 and had an incredible experience. It was a Texas scramble format and the men in our group could not believe how far Marnie could hit the ball. She had an advantage from the women's tees, but consistently drove her tee shot past the men. This was her game, and she was good at it.

With Marnie's diagnosis in early 2013, and with her many chemo infusions, we returned to Joe's tournament in September of that year. This time it had a different feeling—for me and, it's accurate to say, for Marnie. The tournament became more personal. Gone were the long accurate hits off the tee, but that was completely secondary; the act of participation, and the cause, came first and foremost. Numbness in Marnie's fingers and toes was ever-present. But she never complained—not even a hint of discomfort—and she never gave up. She approached every shot with a smile on her face in the hopes that it would be better than the last; the same way that she approached her treatment regimen with cancer. Forever an optimist.

This strong trait of hers, optimism, is perhaps something one is born with, and then adds to. I can appreciate not everyone might feel so energized and upbeat. Surrounding yourself with friends, appreciating each progression, seeing the beauty in yourself, your relationships—and often working on improving them—all contribute to extending life, tolerating treatment, and moving positively and confidently along the path of the cancer journey. I've learned this is important regardless of whether you are the patient, caregiver, or friend, or professional.

What the professionals did.

They congratulated Marnie. They were astounded and shared their astonishment with us. It was wonderful to see them celebrate successes; that helped us tremendously. It reminded us they were human too. Yes, as scientists they might relish in getting a diagnosis right, and predicting or finding a tumour or a strain of illness, but ultimately they didn't want that disease in a fellow human. This was made evident by ongoing compassion.

The professionals in our sphere pushed the envelope—through encouragement and suggestion of treatments—to help toward healing.

BRIAN: The Physicians were amazed at Marnie's stamina. They verbalized it often. On one occasion in a conversation with Dr. Ogaranko, Marnie expressed that she was feeling a little tired; not quite herself after recent chemo treatment. The doctor asked her about her recent activities and she responded that she only had the energy to make three out of her four curling games that week! The doctor was amazed, then explained that a person of normal health would experience some fatigue with this level of exercise.

But, Marnie had high expectations and felt that this should not going to slow her down.

Curling was certainly one of her passions. She took the game seriously and loved to compete. Her teams were successful; won their club championship on a couple of occasions.

Albeit the spirit of the game drove her, the companionship kept her there. She loved curling with her friends. She spoke fondly of curling with her Auntie Maxine. Curling nights became a sanctuary for her. She was doing what she loved to do, with the people she loved. It was a time out from her reality.

THREE STARS

- **Stretch yourself**: create a bucket list, but first, understand your reasons for a bucket list. (If the thought of making one stresses you out, then don't create one.)
- **Contract your horizons**: zoom in on interesting and new views of your surroundings—for example the wonders of nature in grass growing between the concrete.
- **Expand your horizons**: look at the bigger picture: find material to widen your scope—read or watch intelligent documentaries about life and philosophy, about healing and rebirth, and don't be afraid to read about death and dying.

JUNIOR LEAGUE: MADISON

On vacation, when we were tubing in Cass Lake, Minnesota, her hat blew off and everyone could see her bald head. She was so embarrassed and kept apologizing to me. But I didn't care as long as she was comfortable.

OVERTIME

http://www.theguardian.com/lifeandstyle/2012/sep/26/
bucket-lists-are-they-good-idea

Ted Talk: What really matters in life and death. B.J. Miller
https://www.youtube.com/watch?v=apbSsILLh28

PLAYER PROFILE:

(taken directly and chronologically from the eulogy and shared over the chapters of this book)

"Perhaps Marnie's biggest accomplishment was to get me to go camping. While I like to be outdoors, the comfort of a nice bed is important to me. My work colleagues will sometimes refer to me as "Fairmont Foreman" knowing that I enjoy these essentials.

We started camping in a tent and, after Claude and Stacey's wedding in Medicine Hat, ventured on to camp in Canmore and Jasper with Kelly and Amy and Martin and Edie. Other than the threat of grizzly bears and the associated fears—because we'd be sleeping in a soft sided structure —this was a very good experience.

When the children came, camping was something she wanted us to do more of. After many discussions, she convinced me to purchase a pop up trailer. This trailer was an absolute lemon. I am not sure if Larry and Leanne Maykutt are here today, but they can verify these stories. The trailer leaked like a sieve.

On many occasions when it rained, it was dryer outside. It did, however, provide us with great memories. We pulled this trailer to Drumheller, Kananaskis, Hamiota, Buffalo Point, West Hawk, and Cass Lake. We were easy to spot once set up. We were the camper with the big blue tarp over it and us.

We graduated from a pop up camper to a 30 foot travel trailer, complete with kitchen, bathroom, queen-sized bed, fridge, stove, and microwave. Now this was camping! I had finally found a way to bring the Fairmont with us.

River tubing, boat rides, hiking, fishing, movies on the beach, playing cards and board games in the trailer; we had many great times with so many wonderful families while camping.

Thank you Maykutts, Legarys, Juras, Duecks, Crocketts, Bryants, Males, Brooks, Hawkins, Browns, and Gerritsens for all of the great times.

You all know the campfire will not be the same without her."

Second Period
2014

Eight

PLAY BY PLAY

March 11, 2014

Greetings Team Marnie,

Hoping everyone has endured the long winter and is looking forward to the spring season. We certainly are. Our lives continue to be full of many activities and accomplishments that make us proud.

In January Madison passed her driver's test and now has her full license. Where has the time gone? She also got herself a part-time job at Crock-a-Doodle, where she helps kids paint their own pottery at birthday parties or other scheduled events. Goes hand-in-hand with her goal of one day becoming a teacher.

I am hoping that some of this hard earned money will end up paying for gas; one can only dream!

In January, Brayden's Twins AA peewee team competed in a 32 team hockey tournament in Regina. This event attracted teams from all over Western Canada, and we are happy to report that their team won the final in a very exciting overtime game against Yorkton. Hopefully we will see the same success though our Winnipeg playoffs.

In our last update, we mentioned that we were going back to see our surgeon, Dr. MacIntosh, to discuss further treatment options. With the positive news from our chemotherapy rounds, Dr. MacIntosh advised us that there was no benefit in going back into the surgical program. Her advice to us was to have an MRI to evaluate the current situation of the original diagnosis in the breast and lymph nodes and to make treatment decisions once we had these results.

In mid-February we headed back to the St. Boniface hospital for Marnie to have her MRI. While waiting patiently, and while both of us were shovelling out from one of our frequent Manitoba winter storms, we received a phone call from Dr. Macintosh with the MRI results.

We were a little taken aback that a physician would be calling us at 7:45 AM in the morning, but we were thrilled with her news. The MRI revealed that there was no evidence of malignancy (cancer) in the breast or lymph nodes following chemotherapy. Definitely happy times with these results!

This was part one of follow-up testing. We then had to wait to have another CT scan on her liver and abdomen to evaluate progress.

On March 4th, this was done. We visited our oncologist this morning (March 11, 2014) to get the results of this test. While the cancer is not gone from her liver, it appears to have stabilized (no growth, or no new nodules). This is, again, great news, and demonstrates that the chemotherapy and current treatment regimen are working for Marnie.

So…Marnie will continue on with her Tamoxifen treatment. Apart from some partial sleep interruption and the odd hot flash, she is tolerating this medication well.

We will continue to have CT scans every three months to monitor her liver, and mammograms will be completed regularly to watch for any potential irregularities.

We will also make arrangements to have her portacath removed so as to make her feel "normal" and eliminate the constant reminders of her chemo treatments.

Marnie is starting to feel like her "old self" again. She is back at her exercise program, and is honing her competitive skills, on the curling rink, four times a week—we "pimped" out a curling stabilizer bar for Marnie to use for her delivery (a pretty pink color with motivational cancer logos embossed)

Much of her "free" time is spent cheering on Madison and Brayden as both kids are now in soccer and hockey playoffs respectively.

What a difference a year can make. We are in a much better place health wise and mentally, and are definitely looking at the glass as "half-full". We are on our way back to living our normal lives and could not be happier. You really don't know how much you appreciate things until they are taken away. Love you all…

Until our next update!

Brian, Marnie, Madison, and Brayden

TIME OUT

"One of the new things people began to find out in the last century was that thoughts—just mere thoughts—are as powerful as electric batteries—as good for one as sunlight is, or as bad for one as poison. To let a sad thought or a bad one get into your mind is as dangerous as letting a scarlet fever germ get into your body. If you let it stay there after it has got in you may never get over it as long as you live…surprising things can happen to any person who, when a disagreeable or discouraged

> *thought comes into his mind, just has the sense to remember in time and push it out by putting in an agreeable determinedly courageous one. Two things cannot be in one place."*

THE SECRET GARDEN — FRANCIS HODGSON BURNETT

RECAP

So we weren't dying with cancer, we were living with cancer. And each time there was a little good news, we celebrated.

Positive test results are a boost to the journey. And they acknowledge the hard work and energy put into enduring the treatments. Any time that can be gained is time when another treatment might come into play; even a cure. It's not irresponsible or unrealistic to believe that a cure will be found. There is progress with treating this disease. Positive results demonstrate this. And, as a whole, we understand that there will be a day when the collective of those diagnosed with cancer will have a plethora of viable options for remission and/ or a cure. It's happened with other diseases, it's already happened within some cancers and, as science progresses, there will be a cure for all.

COACH'S CORNER

What we did to help ourselves.

We had let a lot of time go by without emailing our group. Life became busier and, at that time, the moment or mood did not strike us to communicate in that way. We were carried away with the schedule of school, sports, and spending time with each other and friends. We acknowledged how much time had passed. We celebrated that we had come so far. We kept crossing things off our lists, and we bonded and reminisced.

BRIAN: Arizona has long been one of our favourite places in the US. We'd vacationed there a couple of times earlier in our marriage: one time as a couple on our own, and another time with Marnie's parents when Marnie was pregnant with Madison.

We loved to break the monotony of a Manitoba winter with the predictable heat of the desert.

It was spring break 2014. We were in-between treatments and decided that a trip to some warm weather was just what the doctor ordered. Good friends, Paul and Sherri, had recently purchased a place in Maricopa, and other friends, Brad and Jane, were heading down to stay in their sister and brother-in-law's place.

We had a fabulous time following and cheering on our Winnipeg Jets as they defeated the Phoenix Coyotes. We spent hours at the factory outlet malls, flea markets, and the many Super Targets that the local areas had to offer. No matter where we went, shopping was always a family priority.

We had a great vacation—barbeques and pool parties with our friends were certainly memorable experiences. Reminiscing led to the best medicine of all: laughter. These were our highlights. I'm unsure if Brad, Jane, Paul, Sherri, Troy and Margaret know how much they contributed to our therapy. These loving friends and the mood of the vacation was the perfect prescription for body, mind, and soul.

A poignant memory from this trip was the family hike we took. Marnie was set on hiking. We did our research and decided that the path we would tackle was Hidden Valley to Mormon Trail. When we found it—it was difficult to locate—it was simply spectacular.

I recall it was a hot day. We were prepared with sunscreen, hats, and plenty of water. But I'm not sure we were totally prepared for the steep slopes and *rugged terrain. Marnie had been battling cancer for over a year at this point. She'd been on Taxotere and was still feeling the effects of numbness in her feet. But, up-up-up we climbed, over and under rock formations, through tunnels, around cacti, all the while avoiding and eluding various critters we watched scurry under boulders.*

But she wouldn't quit. Marnie had heard that the top of this trail revealed some of the best views of Phoenix, and so Marnie was determined to see them for herself.

And of course, Marnie was right.

Over four miles of hiking, she conquered the trail, overcame all obstacles, and stood strong as she took in the outstanding views. She was more winded by the striking landscape than exhaustion. And me? More breathless for her beauty than the battle of the trail.

That was Marnie. She had met her goal. We have the pictures to prove it. Perseverance and determination: two words that had come to define her journey and would establish her legacy.

What others did that was helpful.

They respected the lapse in active communication (albeit electronic); there was certainly plenty of in-person connection.

And they continued to ask us what we needed. Their commitment was ongoing.

They also told us what they were doing—but not in a 'see us be amazing people' kind of way. Fundraising, helping others, being there in humble and gentle ways.

What the professionals did.

They ordered tests. Carried out tests. Pored over research. Answered questions. Made suggestions. Gave advice. Offered opinions. Re-tested. Interpreted. And they celebrated with us. After all, independent of their relationship with us (with any of their patients and patients' teams), they were in a relationship with science—their specialties, their passion for medicine, love of research, or knack with technology—and saw all changes as different parts of the cancer puzzle.

JUNIOR LEAGUE: BRAYDEN

Any Jets game she went to you could always see her in her signature Jets game outfit. The Jets sweater and blue jeans. She always had the biggest smile on her face at the games.

THREE STARS

- Review your journey and acknowledge how far you've come.
- Don't stop asking questions: positive tests are not a signal for inaction.
- Party, but not until you drop. Make sure there's no sign of burnout in your key team members.

OVERTIME

Positive ways to manage your cancer journey (and on not comparing):

http://www.cancercenter.com/discussions/blog/the-danger-of-comparison-positive-ways-to-manage-your-cancer-journey/

http://www.cancer.net/coping-with-cancer/caring-loved-one/
how-caregivers-can-take-care-themselves

PLAYER PROFILE

(taken directly and chronologically from the eulogy, and shared over the chapters of this book).

Marnie was an organizer. Everything had a place. Labeled Rubbermaid containers can be found—well placed—throughout our home. She helped us today with her photo presentation, as every single photo that we have ever taken had been placed in photo albums with the dates clearly marked on their side. It was a very therapeutic task as we shared stories and giggled as we went through the years.

Our friends would laugh at our pantry when we lived on Vineland Crescent; frequently referred to it as the bomb shelter. Why in the world would anyone need 13 chocolate cake mixes? Emergency birthday parties? I soon realized that this was not just all for us. When others needed something, they could count on Marnie to have it. She shared with all, and loved to do it.

She hated clutter. We recently did some work in our basement and this was her time to purge. Several trips to the dump later, the mission was accomplished. I think she can rest better now knowing that this job was done.

Nine

PLAY BY PLAY

June 3, 2014

Hello Team Marnie,

Hope you are all doing well after a long winter and cool spring. It really is nice to feel the warm temperatures again. We wanted to provide you all with an update as to Marnie's health. As part of her regular care, she has been going for CT scans every three months to monitor her cancer. Through the past 18 months we have seen great results from her Taxotere treatment in tumour reduction; so much, that they stopped the chemotherapy and initiated Tamoxifen to help stabilize the disease.

Today we had an appointment with Dr. Pitz to review the results from her latest scan. There has been so much positive news around our journey that today's information threw us for quite a loop.

The tests showed that the two large tumours in her liver showed no growth, but two more liver tumours are now present. The scans also revealed the possibilities of small lesions in the lymph nodes and lung.

We are in a bit of shock from this news as Marnie has been feeling great. She has her energy back, has been taking long walks, and has joined a women's golf league at St. Boniface.

As with our initial diagnosis, we will continue to remain positive on the next steps in fighting this disease. Dr. Pitz has stopped the Tamoxifen and has initiated an oral chemotherapy called Xeloda (Capecitabine). Marnie will take this therapy (5 pills twice a day) for two weeks and then have a week of rest in-between.

This cycle will continue until further notice. The scans and MRIs will be done regularly so we can monitor outcomes. This treatment also requires blood-work be done every three weeks so as to monitor her blood levels, and liver and kidney function.

The side effects are not as bad as the Taxotere, but can lead to skin irritations, mouth sores, numbness in the fingers and toes, and fever. This medication does not affect hair loss.

We have asked for your support before, and are asking for your help again.

Please keep us in your thoughts and prayers as we continue this journey to kick cancer in the ass. It will take a couple of days to get over our latest diagnosis but once we do our determination to battle will be as strong as ever.

Once again, cancer has picked the wrong family to mess with!

Much love,

Brian, Marnie, Madison, and Brayden

September 9, 2014

Hello Team Marnie,

Thank you to those that have joined Marnie's team for the "Run for the Cure". We are looking forward to this date and hope we can share our walk with many of our friends.

If you want to join our team, here is the link: Click here to view the team page for Marnie's Mammaries

This summer has been very eventful for us. Although we stayed relatively close to home, it was packed with many adventures with family and friends. Our last update in June was not filled with the news we were hoping for. We saw some cancer show up in new spots, and grow back in places where it once receded. It once again confirmed that this disease is unpredictable and throws you on an emotional roller coaster. As with our initial diagnosis once we got over the shock, we were ready to fight with a new form of chemotherapy.

Marnie has now completed four rounds of oral Xeloda treatment. The first round of treatment went very well as Marnie tolerated the medication and it's expected side effects.

Round two presented a unique challenge for us. Near the end of the two week course Marnie experienced great fatigue, nausea, vomiting, etc.... These adverse effects led us to the Victoria Hospital Emergency department where they ran several tests, gave her many courses of anti-nausea medications and filled her full of I.V. fluids.

All of the tests came back negative, and it was great to see Marnie leave the hospital with some energy. Although she was not able to eat for almost a week, we were able to keep our daily routine of visiting the hospital and getting a fluid top up until she was able to eat again.

After visiting with our G.P. oncologist, Dr. Ogaranko and consulting with our oncologist Dr. Pitz, it was decided that Marnie would stay on Xeloda, but at a reduced dose for another two rounds.

You can never keep a good woman down! Throughout treatment, our summer rambled on. Weekend journeys to friend's cabins, shopping in Fargo, and camping trips to Bemidji and Falcon Lake restored normalcy to our family. A big highlight for us was the preparation and celebration of Marnie's parents, Brian and Gail's, 50th Wedding Anniversary. On August 22nd our extended family met in Carman for a wonderful weekend to commemorate this achievement, a relationship that Marnie and I have emulated over our 21 years together.

This week Marnie had a CT scan to once again monitor the progress of her cancer. We visited Dr. Pitz today to get the results. I mentioned earlier about the roller coaster, well today we are on a high....

The results of the scan were very positive, indicating that the Xeloda is having a positive effect on her treatment. The chest scan revealed that the lung and lymph node tumors have stabilized and have shown no new growth while the liver metastases have decreased in size since the previous scan. We are very happy with the news and will continue on with this treatment with the hope of seeing more success.

Marnie continues to experience the uncomfortable numbness and tingling in her feet and ankles, and sometimes has some difficulty getting up and walking in the morning. This usually occurs for a short time (a couple of minutes) and then she is ready to face the day.

It is great to see her gain her confidence back as she has shed her wigs and is walking around proudly with her new curly hair.

Hard to believe that September is here and that the kids are back in school. Brayden has started grade 8, and Madison is in grade 12 at Sanford Collegiate. Where does the time go? Both are fully engaged in their sporting activities as Brady is in the midst of AAA tryouts and Madison is finishing off her community soccer playoffs and commencing the start of her high school season. No doubt with their mom cheering every step of the way.....

Love you all, and thank you for your continued support.

Brian, Marnie, Madison, and Brayden

October 6, 2014

Hello Team Marnie,

What a great day yesterday and such creative costumes! A little cool to start but once we got going and the sun came out we were able to stay warm.

How do we begin to thank you? We let us say 5720 ways! This is how much Marnie's Mammaries contributed towards the Run for the Cure and the Canadian Breast Cancer Foundation. We are again humbled by all of you who came out to walk (and roll) with our family and for those who gave generously to the cause. Thank you!

Although Marnie's feet were a little sore last night, she feels truly blessed for the love that was shown by you all.

Until our next update,

Brian, Marnie, Madison, and Brayden

TIME OUT

"It has been a terrible, horrible, no good, very bad
day. My mom says some days are like that."

ALEXANDER AND THE TERRIBLE, HORRIBLE, NO
GOOD, VERY BAD DAY —JUDITH VIORST.

RECAP

The news hit us hard. In March it had been all smiles and celebration. Now we faced more challenges. It was like being real playing pieces on a Snakes and Ladders board game.

COACH'S CORNER

What we did to help ourselves.

We cried, grieved, we ranted, we got angry, we shook our heads, we felt defeat as close as our own shadows. And then we regrouped, we armed ourselves with more information, we put on our fighting gloves and our game faces, and we moved forward.

What others did that was helpful.

They cried, they got angry, they ranted, they shook their heads then, they too, regrouped, armed themselves with their superpowers, and moved with us in the direction of healing.

We know that family members worked behind the scenes at anything and everything, including protecting us from seeing their hurt; we know they tried so hard to spare us seeing their pain over our pain.

They also looked for other ways to help us and help others. Madison and her cousin, McKenna, got together and organized a team to participate in the "Run for the Cure". Through their creativity, team "Marnie's Mammaries" was formed, and by word of mouth, and the powers of social media, our team began to grow. It was a truly inspirational day to walk with thousands of people who have all been touched by cancer. You walk with patients, caregivers, their families, and of course the many survivors who have conquered this foe. It was an awesome day.

What the professionals did.

We'd like to think they ranted and shook their heads too. But they knew the medications and the human body. They had experience that we didn't. They reassured us, as best they could. They changed up meds and doses. They provided care to make sure Marnie was hydrated and as comfortable as possible.

In terms of professionals and volunteers, in case you're wondering: here are the organizations which form part of the scenery during a cancer journey.

The **Canadian Breast Cancer Foundation** is a charitable organization. It raises money to advance research, education, diagnosis and treatment of BREAST CANCER.

In 1986, Nancy Tsai (then Nancy Paul) established a foundation to serve as an advocate for education and awareness, early diagnosis and treatment, and quality of life. It is part of a seven-member coalition which funds breast cancer research in Canada.

The Canadian Breast Cancer Foundation is well known for its Canadian Imperial Bank of Commerce (CIBC) Run For The Cure. The Run was created in 1992 by a small number of volunteers to raise awareness and funds. The first event took place in Toronto, where over 1,500 participants raised $85,000. The Run has grown into Canada's largest single-day, volunteer-led fundraising event dedicated to breast cancer research, education, and awareness.

The **Canadian Cancer Society** is a national, community-based charitable organization of volunteers whose mission is to "eradicate and enhance the quality of life of those living with the disease".

The Canadian Cancer Society is the largest national cancer charity and the largest national charitable funder of cancer research in Canada.

The idea for this organization came from the Saskatchewan Medical Association in 1929, in forming Canada's first cancer committee. In 1937, the National Study Committee recommended the formation a of new organization, which was later called Canadian Cancer Society for the control of cancer. In 1938 the 'Society' was formed to educate Canadians about the early warning signs of cancer. It was seen as a necessity—the information—because, at that time, many people did not seek medical help until their cancer was well advanced.

In 1947, the Society began funding cancer research through the creation of the **National Cancer Institute of Canada**, an agreement between the Canadian Cancer Society and the Federal Department of Health and Welfare. The Society continues to fund cancer research today through the Canadian Cancer Society Research Institute.

With national offices in Toronto and Ottawa, and 10 provincial and territorial divisions, the Canadian Cancer Society has approximately 140,000 volunteers and about 1,200 full-time staff.

Their events include: Daffodil Month, Relay For Life, and Cops for Cancer. Each of these main events has a number of 'sub-events'. The fundraising activities are meant to bring awareness, relieve suffering, and move toward the goal of eradicating cancer.

Each Province and Territory has its own branch of cancer services associated with health care. **CancerCare Manitoba** is the provincially mandated cancer agency tasked with providing cancer services to the people of Manitoba. CCMB is responsible for providing care, treatment and support across the entire cancer service spectrum—prevention, early detection, diagnosis, treatment and care, and palliative care.

CancerCare Manitoba works with Manitoba's regional health authorities, the University of Manitoba's Department of Medicine, Diagnostic Services Manitoba and volunteer funding agencies, in particular the CancerCare Manitoba Foundation.

Of two locations in Winnipeg, CCMB's main site is on McDermot Avenue at the Health Sciences Centre campus, and the second is at the St. Boniface Hospital.

Outside Winnipeg, through partnerships with 4 regional health authorities, CCMB provides community based cancer services through the Community Cancer Program (CCP) Network at 16 locations across the province, and cancer support services through a community resource centre in a 17th community, bringing care closer to home for those that live in rural Manitoba.

In addition to serving the province of Manitoba, CCMB also provides some services for populations in the adjacent jurisdictions of Northwestern Ontario, Nunavut, and Saskatchewan.

CancerCare Manitoba employs over 800 staff members and 48 physician specialists, and has an annual operating budget of $102.2 million.

THREE STARS

- When forced to take a step back, keep your balance: hold your ground at each setback; refuse to take two steps back.
- Continue to look for trials, and ask questions about current medications
- Cry, rant, get angry, shake your head, but please regroup.

JUNIOR LEAGUE: BRAYDEN

My Mom always loved to watch me and Maddy's sporting events and, no matter what, she would be the loudest and most proud parent in the stands. No matter how sick or tired she was, she wouldn't miss one of our events for the world.

JUNIOR LEAGUE: MADISON

Winnipeg Goldeyes games with Brayden, Canada vs USA Women's World Cup soccer with Grandma Gail and Grandpa Brian, and the Winnipeg Jets "white out" playoff game. Mom always wanted to take a 'selfie'. I was so embarrassed!

OVERTIME

The advances and setbacks in a cancer journey

http://www.cedars-sinai.edu/About-Us/News/News-Releases-2014/Finding-Meaning-in-the-Cancer-Journey.aspx

The way chemotherapy can affect day-to-day thinking

http://www.cedars-sinai.edu/Patients/Programs-and-Services/Cancer-Survivorship-and-Rehabilitation/Emerging-from-the-Haze-Chemobrain-Rehabilitation-Program.aspx

PLAYER PROFILE

(taken directly and chronologically from the eulogy and shared over the chapters of this book)

"Marnie loved sports. She was a very accomplished athlete through her high school years. She excelled at Basketball, Cross Country, Curling, Fastball, Golf, Ringette,

Track and Field, and Volleyball. She was the captain of many of her teams, and competed at the provincial level in many of her activities.

She loved the competition. Many of the letters that have come in since her passing have been from people who have played with and against Marnie. They talk about her respect for the game and her opponents; her strong display of sportsmanship, her friendly disposition during all events. They also said not to confuse this with her strong desire to win.

Her recent passion was curling. She managed to do this four times a week through last winter. She looked forward to these games as it was a chance to be with her friends. She developed many relationships through the Wildwood and Pembina Curling Clubs. I have not met all of you, but I feel that I know you through all of the stories she has relayed to me over the years.

She loved curling with Auntie Maxine and her team. With no disrespect to the age of your team, she fit right in; curling was your bond and she spoke very highly of your time on the ice and through your many lunch time functions.

I mention the age because of a time I needed to get hold of Marnie for of one her many tests she had to have done. The time of her appointment had changed and I knew she was curling. I phoned the Pembina Curling Club and, when the ice maker answered, I told him that I needed to reach my wife. He'd wanted to know the name of her team, of which I had no idea. Just as he was telling me he couldn't help, I said, "She will be the youngest one on the ice." He chuckled and said, "I know exactly who she is." Safe to say she arrived at her appointment on time.

She loved to watch and study curling on television. As soon as the Scotty's, the Briar, the World Championships, or any bonspiel came on the television, we all knew best not to bother Marnie. It was fun to watch her give Jennifer Jones and Jeff Stoughton (both individuals with the status of World Curling Champions) advice through the television, while questioning their strategies."

Ten

PLAY BY PLAY

December 2, 2014

Hello Team Marnie,

It truly is hard to believe that it is coming up on two years since Marnie's initial diagnosis.

Although, we have never become comfortable with this routine, we continue to accept and appreciate the generous support of Marnie's medical contingent, and the continuous love from her "TEAM".

This was evident with your support in this year's Walk for the Cure and "Marnie's Mammaries".

A final total of $6,070 was achieved. WOW! Thanks again to all the participants who came out to walk in Winnipeg or their local communities and to all who donated to this event. Much Love!

Marnie and I met again today with Dr. Pitz. He once again greeted us with a huge smile and in his words "great results".

A sense of relief and a chance to breathe! The past three months Marnie has continued her Zeloda treatments and she is responding well. Her recent CT scans demonstrated no changes in her tumor sizes. That is, they are stable, and no new lesions were found.

Although Marnie was a little disappointed in these results (she was hoping for tumor size reduction), Dr. Pitz provided an explanation that no change is good news. We agree...

So, what's next??? Marnie will start another round of Zeloda tomorrow. These treatments last for 14 days, followed by a week of rest. Her doctors have slowly been increasing her dose and she continues to tolerate this therapy well. In consultation with both Dr. Pitz and Dr. Ogaranko they are hoping that Marnie will receive another 30-40 courses of this therapy. No one said this was going to be a short journey, and we are certainly up for the challenge...

After two years, you would expect a spirit to become somewhat broken, or at times weaken. This is not the case as Marnie's outlook and positivity shine daily.

She continues to curl four times a week, and gains much pride from cheering on Madison in indoor soccer, and Brayden at the rink. She has volunteered for Madison's grad committee and just helped in the production of 1500 holiday wreaths as a fundraiser. All is good...

**"Christmas, my child, is love in action. Every time
we love, every time we give, it's Christmas."**

DALE EVANS

'Tis the season for holiday spirit. We wish you all a healthy and happy holiday season, and thank you all again for making every day feel like Christmas for us.

Until our next update,

Brian, Marnie, Madison, and Brayden

TIMEOUT

"Sometimes it's like people are a million times more beautiful to you in your mind. It's like you see them through a special lens— but maybe if it's how you see them, that's how they really are."

THE SUMMER I TURNED PRETTY —JENNY HAN.

RECAP

It's true that she really kept that positive attitude. Two years in and she was all about the letter P: Positive, Persistent, Powerful, Personable, Profoundly Perfect, and totally *PEED* off about cancer getting in the way of our lives.

Oh, and of course, Purchasing. Retail therapy continued.

COACH'S CORNER

What we did to help ourselves.

After the race we celebrated Thanksgiving and moved on to the festivities of Christmas. Medication aside, Marnie was not going to let cancer affect sports or seasonal celebrations.

Our house was one of the first to have the lights up, and our tree one of the first ones decorated. Christmas was a year-round event. As soon as one was over, the next started. It was a chance to address her two addictions: family and shopping! Sales were to be had, and deals to be made. We'd stumble on various gifts hidden under beds, in closets, or in the basement, waiting to be wrapped for next year's Noel. This was a system of healing for her. 'If I can shop and buy it, I will be there to see someone get it'; medicine comes in all forms.

What others did that was helpful.

Sounds like a broken record, but they celebrated with us. They worked to make things easier. Dropping off food, taking extra care to see if we needed anything. Kept it as normal as possible—why change a great thing?

What the professionals did.

Cancer does not stop for Christmas or any other holiday a family celebrates, and therefore the medical professionals do not stop either. Monitoring the medication was important, no matter the season, and our doctor was available—and totally aware—that Marnie had exceeded all outcomes and tolerated her treatments with unparalleled strength. Still, they were realistic, heeded warnings about side effects, and offered their expertise; gave their hearts and souls to their work and therefore us.

> *BRIAN: I mentioned at the beginning, bonds form with all professionals involved. We had clinicians' e-mail addresses and cellphone numbers. We never abused the privilege. We also established lines of communication over issues like new clinical trials or the need for a change in a prescription.*
>
> *During the worst period, when we were having a hard time managing pain, I exchanged text messages with Dr. Ogaranko. He was unable to send a prescription to the pharmacy (for our next step in pain management) due to provincial protocols. I had to see him in person. He gave me his address like any caring friend would.*
>
> *Karma is a funny thing. When Dr. Ogaranko gave me his address I recognized it as being the house right next door to the house that I grew up in. I'd spent 20 years of my life there; it was the last home my mother lived in.*
>
> *It was a Sunday morning when I arrived at his house. His kids were still asleep, and he was waiting for me with a medication to help Marnie get through her discomfort.*

There I stood, on his doorstep—I could touch a thousand memories by stepping onto the next front lawn. Family times, childhood, my mother's cancer journey. Somehow I hoped that between the stars aligning and these new pain pills that our healing journey would change. And, you know what? I'm grateful for those serendipitous moments that pushed us forward, along, up, and beyond.

THREE STARS

- Prepare for flexibility. Have a plan B and C in mind for holiday visits or hosting others. That way, 'if' something happens there's an alternative for all family members.
- Continue to schedule rest—you may be a champion, but even superstars have to rest. Don't wait to NEED it, take it when you feel well.
- Reminisce, get emotional, turn up the music, turn down the music, do whatever you need to do, without apology.

JUNIOR LEAGUE: MADISON

Shopping! Florida, Grand Forks, and Fargo. Even Winnipeg. She taught me how to be a responsible shopper. This was one of my favourite things to do with Mom. Even if she was tired, she would do anything to go and buy some new clothes.

Grad dress shopping – Grandma Gail, Mom, and I. I ended up buying the first dress that I tried on. We went back for many fittings and after taking in 6 ½ inches it finally fit. Mom always made me drive because she was too tired. But she was a trooper. I am happy that I got to experience this with her.

JUNIOR LEAGUE: BRAYDEN

Whenever my cousins would come into the city they always wanted to shop and, since I wasn't old enough to stay home alone, Mom would always drag me to the mall with them. She would try to keep my spirits high and make me have fun, although it really would never work. Sorta. Kinda. Actually, shopping with Mom was fun. She would get mad at me because I'm not very responsible with money when it comes to buying clothes. I would never look for the good deal. With Mom, she wouldn't buy anything unless it was on sale.

OVERTIME

Seasonal articles:

http://www.cancercare.org/publications/55-coping_with_cancer_during_the_holidays

http://www.cancer.net/blog/2013-12/five-ideas-maintaining-your-holiday-cheer

PLAYER PROFILE

(taken directly and chronologically from the eulogy and shared over the chapters of this book)

"Marnie loved doing puzzles, riding roller coasters, tubing behind a boat, walking with friends, shopping, tulips, and daisies. But most of all she loved her family.

She had a very special relationship with her mom and dad. She was happiest driving out to Carman to spend time with Brian and Gail. Whether it was for Thanksgiving, a game of golf, or just a chance to visit, these times were very special to Marnie. She was thankful of the life 'you, her parents' provided and the opportunities that came with it. She was an only child, and watching the bond between these three was remarkable.

Marnie was an only child by birth, but she had plenty of siblings. This was thanks to Russ and Hazel Cumming of Lenore, Manitoba, and the four daughters they created: Maxine, Gail, Lauree, and Carol. They all went on to have children of their own, and this became Marnie's infrastructure. Brock, Martin, Kellee, Kathy, and Karma became more than cousins to her. They were her brothers and sisters, her protectors, her confidantes, and best friends.

Marriages added more to the family as Michelle, Edie, Curtis, Warren and Doug and I soon benefited from the closeness of this group. We spent many amazing times together over the holidays, at family reunions, camping, visits to Hamiota and Portage La Prairie and, lest we forget, 617 Kilkenny Drive—a very special home where we have spent the last couple of evenings reminiscing of our times together and raising a glass to Marnie. She loved you all."

Las Vegas our new "normal"

Team "Fight Like a Girl" – Manitoba Marathon Relay Team

Brayden's Hockey Helmet- Supporting his mom on the ice…..

Our last family picture- Madison's High School Graduation

The magic of Tahiti – our "bucket list" destination

Marnie's Mammaries; our Run for the Cure team!

Madison helping to cut of Marnie's Pigtails …..an emotional day for us all

Part of our Miles for Marnie Manitoba Marathon running/fundraising team

"Pimping out" Marnie's curling stabilizer to help with the balance in her delivery.

The view from the top on our hike in Phoenix. Pure determination…..

2015
Third Period

Eleven

PLAY BY PLAY

March 3, 2015

Hello Team Marnie,

We hope you have all experienced a healthy and prosperous start to your year. Thank you again for all of your support. If you don't want to be included in future updates, please let me know.

We have been thankful for many positive experiences to start 2015. On January 11th we accompanied many friends at a surprise event (Happy B-Day Sharon) and joined Soup Sisters/Broth Brothers to help Osborne House make meals for families affected by domestic violence. Over 90 litres of soup were made! A great event for an even better cause.

The following weekend we were off to Minneapolis for the Minnesota Wild Hockey Tournament. Brayden and his Monarch Team were very successful, going 7-0 and bringing home the championship banner! Their team finished their own league play in first place with a 28-2 record and are now competing in the AAA playoffs. Go Monarchs Go!

Madison has been extremely busy balancing her soccer and work schedule with school and her grade 12 Math and English provincial exams. Through

---

all of this, her application to University of Winnipeg was successful. She has been accepted to and will be starting at the Faculty of Education in the fall. She will make an excellent teacher! We are very proud of their accomplishments.

"When you hit that unexpected bump in the road, remember that it is only a bump, not a mountain. Go over it or around it but make sure you keep going"

~ DEB SHAPIRO

Today, we hit one of these bumps in our journey. After several months of stability with Xeloda treatment, the liver tumor has shown some growth. The largest cancer mass has enlarged from the previous scan and has gone from a 1.8 x 2.0 cm size to 4.4 to 4.2 cm. This caught us off guard. Marnie looks and feels great. She has tremendous amounts of energy and continues to be very involved in her weekly activities.

We went into today with very high hopes and these results did not make sense to us.

Once again, we are reminded of the unpredictability of this disease.

Through this journey, you really don't have the occasion to feel sorry for yourself. You take the time you need to laugh, smile, and celebrate success and/or lament and have a good cry through the adversity. The decision making is rapid as you move onto your next phase of your journey.

Our next trek in getting around this bump will be to change our treatment regimen to a drug called Eribulin. This moves us from pills back to intravenous chemo therapy. We will start this immediately (this week) and continue on until further notice.

This treatment is initiated on day one, and then repeated eight days after.

There is a rest period of seven days and then day one starts again.

Our oncologist tells us that this drug is well tolerated (some extremity numbness, and fatigue) and that Marnie should generally feel well through these regimens.

Marnie will have her blood levels checked every three weeks, and treatment outcomes will be monitored by a CT scan every three months.

We will do this…while the news is still fresh, we will continue to approach every day with positivity and the will to beat this disease. We will keep going….

> **"Friendship isn't a big thing — it's
> a million little things."**
>
> **~AUTHOR UNKNOWN**

We thank you for your friendship and all of your many acts of kindness. For without you, we could not get through this.

Until our next update,

Brian, Marnie, Madison, and Brayden

June 3, 2015

Hello Team Marnie,

We hope that you are all doing well and are enjoying what Spring has to offer…

We have had quite a wild ride since our last communication. In early March, Marnie started on a new drug called Eribulin. This is a newer agent for the treatment of metastatic breast cancer. Things were going well with treatment until we were presented with yet another challenge; the liver tumor was putting pressure on her bile ducts, closing them off, and thus affecting the performance of its function.

With this, Marnie was taken off chemotherapy for about a month and underwent a procedure called and MRCP (magnetic resonance cholangiopancreatography). This is an invasive procedure where they place stents in the liver ducts via a scope.

We are happy that the process worked, her jaundice disappeared and chemo was once again initiated. This is one tough lady! A very emotional time as Marnie once again experienced the unwanted side effect of complete hair loss.

Throughout these endeavors we continue to enjoy life and celebrate success.

March was a very good month as Brady's Monarch team won their city hockey championship. Congratulations to the boys on a great season and this well-deserved win.

Spring break took us to Florida where we enjoyed a very relaxing vacation with friends. It was great to get away, feel the warm sun, the soft sand and enjoy the ocean. We loved the dinners, the visits, the fishing and the boat rides accompanied by many local dolphins. Thanks guys!

Lest we forget the shopping! Thank goodness for luggage weight restrictions on airlines...

Madison has been very busy through all of this preparing for her grade 12 graduation. The dress is bought and altered, and hair styles have been tested and approved. She also recently won her coach's award for soccer at the recent high school salute. Very proud of her accomplishments. She has truly come a long way...

April saw us cheering on the Winnipeg Jets and their first playoff experience since re-joining the NHL. Marnie and I were able to get to both home games to witness the excitement of the city, and the energy displayed at the MTS Centre. Something we will never forget. Go Jets Go!

Yesterday we received some very mixed news from our oncologist. While some of Marnie's tumors have shrunk, the largest one in her liver has grown substantially. This growth has our physician changing our course again.

This Friday we will start a chemotherapy referred to as FEC. It is a combination of Fluorouracil (5FU), epirubicin, and cyclophosphamide. It is generally well tolerated.

The biggest side effects are hair loss (already done), and nausea. This chemotherapy will require Marnie to have a port again—installed for medicine delivery.

This port procedure will occur sometime over the next three weeks.

We have spoken to our oncologist about future plans and we have many options. While surgery is out of the question, the possibility of radiation exists.

The Winnipeg Regional Health Authority has recently purchased new equipment that can specialize in radiating the liver. Our oncologist is going to recommend us for a trial as we wait patiently to see if we are proper candidates for this procedure.

We also have many other chemo options available and many new therapies are on their way.

> **"We constantly wait in anticipation for
> a miracle to happen in our life unaware
> that the miracle is actually life itself"**
>
> **~DANIEL CHIDIAC**
>
> A friend of mine reminded me today that miracles can happen… Thanks for your perspective. We believe they can and are in the process of praying for one.
>
> Love to you all,
>
> Until our next update,
>
> Brian, Marnie, Madison, and Brayden

TIMEOUT

> *"You know how you let yourself think that everything will be all right if you can only get to a certain place or do a certain thing. But when you get there you find it's not that simple."*
>
> **WATERSHIP DOWN— RICHARD ADAMS.**

RECAP

We knew some of what we were in for in January 2013, when we'd received the initial diagnosis. We were further stunned when a secondary cancer was diagnosed. And we'd made such progress. Now, we were faced with some real-time devastation.

Can anyone prepare for a certain type of ending, knowing that in the preparing one might be bending the rules of positive thinking?

Is it okay to have a conversation about 'the end' when those words might alter the course of what will be?

How does one plan to say goodbye without that planning affecting the vision of a remission of miraculous proportion?

There is no satisfactory answer that we have found other than to put one foot in front of another, one thought at a time, and love deeply in the moment.

COACH'S CORNER

What we did to help ourselves.

Spring Break. We went away. We crossed more items off our bucket list. After all, we only have the now—and never had that been more evident. If happiness and time with friends and family was the best therapy, then that is exactly what we would do. And we did. From comfort food to shopping therapy, from laughter to tears, we took a Spring Break holiday to a warm place with even warmer hearts.

> *BRIAN: That vacation, to Mark and Sharon's home in Anna Maria Island, Florida, was meant to bring respite, and attempt to restore a little normalcy to challenging times.*
>
> *It's a place of pristine beaches, aquamarine water, fantastic food, and a wonderful community with a 'small town' feel. One can drive, walk, bike, or travel by our favourite way: golf cart.*

About ten days before we left, Marnie was showing signs of fluid retention in her abdomen, and her skin appeared quite yellow.

Dr. Ogaranko, at the Victoria Hospital, definitely felt it was a sign of early jaundice, but wanted to run some tests to understand the reason for the fluid retention.

It was off for another MRI, which took place a couple of days prior to leaving on our trip. We hoped we could get the results. Dr. Allan Micflikier was our consulting physician to whom we spoke daily—should we go to Florida, should we not go to Florida? Through careful consultation, we left Winnipeg and made our way south.

During our time there we spent treasured hours with friends, and we poked around the various shops, checked out the stately homes along the coast and canals, and did lots of people watching.

On one particular day I happened to notice I'd missed several calls from a Manitoba area code. When I called the number, Dr. Micflikier answered. He told me they'd done a deeper dive on Marnie's tests and found the reason for her abdominal edema (the fluid retention in her abdomen). The tumours were growing and blocking her bile ducts. That is, the tumours were not allowing the liver to perform its function properly.

He told me he wanted to see us in his office on the Monday when we were home so he could arrange for Marnie to have a procedure to stent the liver ducts (in order to open them so the liver could perform normal functions). In addition, he shared with me that the MRI showed shading in her spine. Yes, the cancer had spread and was now in her bones.

There is a point where, as caregiver and communicator, one walks a fine line. Should this have been Marnie on the phone with the doctor? Should I have located her and then we could have taken the call together?

Our relationship was one of trust and within that trust we had established certain roles in the cancer journey. It's essential to talk with those closest about the roles.

In that moment, on the phone call which I had returned, I made those decisions—or perhaps the decision was made for me in less than an instant as I noticed the area code and made the missed call, not knowing it would be that doctor, or any doctor.

I was speechless. Here we were in what seemed like paradise, for the specific reason of a little respite, and now there was more news. Of course I knew the overall situation, we hadn't lived with cancer for these years without knowing the various outcomes, but we'd hoped for a little break from our day-to-day challenges. Should I tell her?

She was having a great time. Surrounded by family and friends in a wonderful place, she was thoroughly enjoying the break.

It was early in the trip. I decided not to ruin the rest of her break.

As a caregiver, spouse, and partner this was a burden of staggering proportion on many levels. What happens if it gets worse throughout the week? Had I balanced responsibility responsibly?

The decision to travel down to Florida had been approved by our medical team. But, ultimately, I'd now been placed in a difficult position. I was out of my element. We weren't in Canada. I didn't know the system. Who were the local doctors? Where should we go if her symptoms increased? It seemed like I'd failed by not planning for unforeseen circumstances. Had I slipped? Was I losing it? Did I have a healthy perspective?

Though I loved the people we were with and enjoyed the place we were staying, Monday afternoon could not come soon enough.

We returned on Monday. I did not tell Marnie about the results until we were in the parking lot across from Dr. Micflikier's office.

Would you have done the same?

Everyone's journey is unique. We were into our third year and we'd gone through a lot together, and we'd each gone through our own personal version of a lot—though I would have traded places with her in a heartbeat.

And so, another hard conversation. I explained, in the parking lot, that I'd not wanted to ruin her time away. I'd wanted her to enjoy every moment of her Florida experience. I justified that I had made the decision so that both of us didn't need to lose our minds.

And, she understood. She said she appreciated it. And we got out of the car and went to challenge our emotions and minds once again.

We met with the doctor, came up with a plan, and Marnie had the procedure—which resulted in a successful outcome. Then we carried on with our scheduled treatment modality.

What others did that was helpful.

Friends and family were close by, continuing with what they did best: 'friendship'. Their dedication was inspirational. Their understanding and demonstration of comprehension of the 'news' and 'our ongoing hope' kept us as steady as we could be.

BRIAN: I've mentioned I work in the Healthcare industry. My employer and contacts can be counted twofold in 'what others did that was helpful' and 'what the professionals did'.

Throughout our cancer experience I spoke with many people that I work with about Marnie's condition, her updates, her medications, and options for future therapies. I picked their brains to learn about new advances in the field of oncology. I communicated these to Marnie on a regular basis. These amazing 'professionals, colleagues, people' supplied us with questions to ask, tips on how avoid some of the unwanted side effects of medicines, and confidence that we were on the right path; they were in our corner. I appreciate all of their input.

I would like to thank Kris for the time he dedicated to my queries, the speed of his responses, his genuine compassion, deep sense of empathy, and for his friendship. **You are truly in the right position for what you do in our organization; they are fortunate to have you.**

What the professionals did.

They kept going with what they knew, what they discovered; total dedication with every ounce of their souls.

Tireless research from those we did not even know, working on behalf of all people who have cancer, takes place in labs all over the world. All scientists who work on various branches—from genetics *to* immunology; nutrition *to* aging; technology in developing diagnostics *to* surgical techniques—each have a stake in unravelling the mysteries of the disease.

Though it may not have dawned on us at each doctor's visit or test, on reflection, we were aware that for every person diagnosed with cancer there are hundreds if not thousands working on a patient's behalf. It's staggering to consider the investment of money, time, and brainpower that goes into the entire spectrum of this disease.

As one is amazed at the strength of a body—in our case, particularly Marnie's— and struck by the reality of the pervasive nature of cancer, there is a strange kind of awe regarding it.

While we revered those whose passion is to find and place pieces of the puzzle, we began to understand why those people go into that kind of work. What a mammoth challenge, a considerable slice of responsibility, and a magnanimous sense of duty each professional must feel. And, what a steadfast and unwavering personality trait each must possess in order to witness the devastating effects on patients they see face-to-face, weekly, daily, and sometimes hourly.

THREE STARS

- If you haven't had 'the talk' or 'made the plan' do so. It doesn't mean you've given up.
- Care for the caregivers, self-care, and ease up on some routines. Now's the time to cut a little more slack.
- Share with family and friends as you wish; you own this time. Do whatever you need to on your terms.

JUNIOR LEAGUE: MADISON

We were both very emotional. We would sit on the couch together and cry over Ellen, The Biggest Loser, or Say Yes to the Dress, all the while eating chocolate ice cream and feeling guilty.

BRIAN:

Marnie and I had so many conversations about life during her last few months.

We were still very hopeful that things would turn around, but we were also very realistic about the situation.

We reminisced about our past, recalling stories about how we met, our first date, and our wedding day.

We talked about our many vacations together, the birth of our children, and how proud we were of their accomplishments.

We spoke about what life would look like if she was gone. I hated having this conversation; actually refused to have it on several occasions.

To me it was like I was giving up on her.

To her it was the need to plan; the need to ensure that everything would be okay if she did succumb to cancer.

These were not easy discussions. They were filled with tears as we spoke about our dreams of our kids going to University, their dreams, and how we could help make them a reality.

We spoke about her parents and how we would look after them.

We spoke about our finances and what we wanted to leave to our children.

We spoke about how lucky we were to have found each other, and how thankful we were to spend the time that we did together.

We never felt sorry for ourselves.

These were very honest discussions based on the life that we had created. We were proud of what we had accomplished, both good and bad, and celebrated our achievements.

OVERTIME

On the depth of research on cancer:

https://nccih.nih.gov/health/cancer/camcancer.htm

http://www.helpguide.org/harvard/dealing-with-a-loved-ones-serious-illness.htm

PLAYER PROFILE

(taken directly and chronologically from the eulogy and shared over the chapters of this book)

"Madison and Brayden you were her world. There is nothing that Mom would not have done for you; a warm smile, a big hug, an ear to listen to, or a shoulder to cry on. Mom was always there.

She loved watching you both play sports. Whether it was hockey or soccer, you could always count on Mom volunteering her time to make sure all players were taken to the game.

When she was there you could not help but hear her cheering from the stands for her children and the effort of the other athletes. It was loud, it was often, it might not have been politically correct, but it was honest.

I joked with her last year when Hockey Manitoba made it mandatory for at least one parent to take a "Respect in Sport" course prior to Brayden being able to register for hockey. The goal of this program is to raise awareness on how we are behaving at the arena and how we should all be respecting the game, its players, coaches and officials.

For those that see me at a game, I am usually by myself or with a couple of parents who stand quietly in the corner of the rink. We rarely say a word if not to each other.

When it came time to take the course there was 'no way' she was going to do it. This hurdle was in 'no way' going to stop her from speaking her mind and perhaps letting a referee know what she thought of him.

Needless to say I was on the computer that night, and Marnie carried on supporting the kids in her usual fashion.

Being the teacher that Marnie was, she loved attending parent teacher night for her kids. She beamed with pride as she heard of your classroom accomplishments, the respect you demonstrated to your teachers and fellow students, and how hard you worked to achieve your grades. These values were very important to Mom. It gave validation to her that you were on the right path, and the combination of what you were learning at school and the life lessons at home were shaping you into good people.

She was so proud of both Madison and Brayden as they entered into the next phase of their school careers; Brayden entering Shaftesbury High School, and Madison in the Faculty of Education at University of Winnipeg—go figure, a teacher just like her mom."

Twelve

PLAY BY PLAY

> **"Mindfulness is about love and loving life.
> When you cultivate this love, it gives you
> clarity and compassion for life, and your
> actions happen in accordance with that."**
>
> **– JON KABAT-ZINN**

Over the past two and a half years, we have spent many hours in clinics, at various tests and procedures, in the hospital, or at chemotherapy. The one thing that we are constantly amazed at is how happy and nice everyone is to each other.

These are people that live their days in fear, uncertainty, and rely on a sense of hope to get them through the day, yet they find the time to smile, to say hello, to support you, and to wish you luck along your journey. It is a true brotherhood/sisterhood and is incredibly inspirational.

We bring this up not as a lesson, but as a realization that is lost; even in the toughest times, and through all of this adversity, there is a sense of compassion and kindness that shines through. It makes us smile, gives us optimism, and helps get us through the next hour, day, or week. It is one of the key takeaways that we have gleaned through this experience, and one that we are trying to take outside of the Cancer community.

Since our last update we continue to face life head on and have had many great experiences.

Madison graduated from Sanford Collegiate in June and was the recipient of many scholarships for her academic achievements.

Brayden officially closed the door on his junior high days at HGI.

We're very proud of them both for their commitment to school, and the grades that they achieved.

Over the summer we have had the opportunity for many great visits with friends and family. Visits to Hamiota, Jessica Lake, Lake of the Woods, and Ditch Lake have certainly been highlights.

It was wonderful to get caught up and to see everyone. Great times, great food, and many laughs. Thanks for your hospitality!

August saw our annual trip to Cass Lake Minnesota. We ventured down with five families from Winnipeg for seven days to experience the hospitality of Stony Point Resort. Boating, tubing, fishing, basketball, Zorba's, and the beach were all highlights from this vacation.

Right now we are in the midst of some home renovations. While we were in Hamiota, and with the help of Uncle Doug, we stripped some structures and went home with a load of reclaimed wood. This has been quite the process. It is now milled and we have created two feature walls in the basement. Looks great! We are also in the process of completing a remodel of the kids' bathroom. Thanks to Gord H. for all your help on this project.

With all of this positivity, we wish we had better news to share with you. Today we visited our oncologist to get the results of Marnie's CT scan that she had last Friday, and to establish the effectiveness of her new chemo-therapy…Very mixed results. While the large tumor in her liver did not grow, several new smaller ones have emerged. This is of concern to Dr. Pitz and we will once again change our course of therapy.

We have several options to consider. These being Methotrexate, or another form of Taxotere which Marnie had success with earlier. We are also working with Dr. Pitz to see if we can gain access to a new drug called 'Palbociclib' through special authorization with the Canadian government, or through a clinical trial.

Stay tuned…

Another option for therapy is Liver radiation. This has been up and run-ning in Winnipeg now for two weeks. We were contacted last Friday by Dr. Nashed and are currently waiting on a consult date for this process.

Many options still exist for us. We will continue to go through this with a smile on our faces, and will sneak all the positivity we can from our friends, family, and other cancer patients that we meet along the way. Whoever said don't sweat the small stuff could not have been more right!

Until our next update,

Brian, Marnie, Madison, and Brayden

"As Hagrid had said, what would come would come and he would have to meet it when it did."

HARRY POTTER AND THE GOBLET OF FIRE — J.K. ROWLING.

Our yearly trip to Cass Lake, Minnesota was always fun. In Cass Lake – that was when Mom was the happiest. Mom would always over-pack so she would never run out of anything. Mom was always the life around the campfire and be the last one at the fire every night, except this year when she was very tired and had to go to bed early.

~BRAYDEN

I just wish . . . I always think about how she won't be there on my wedding day.

-MADISON

Thirteen

Hello Team Marnie,

Almost three years ago we were hit with the devastating news that Marnie had developed breast cancer. We were further alarmed (a short time later) when we discovered that the disease had metastasized to her liver.

The news yesterday hit us pretty much the same way.

Over the past three or four weeks, Marnie has been in great discomfort. She has been experiencing much pain and swelling in her stomach and in her words, "felt like she was nine months pregnant".

We had visited her doctor on many occasions to manage the pain, and to have the fluid drained from the stomach region. This past weekend, all symptoms escalated to the point where she was so swollen she could not walk 10 steps without losing her breath. The pain was very hard to manage; another new prescription was initiated. This worked sporadically and got to a point where comfort was not an option.

Yesterday we went for more tests and found out that the cancer had over-taken her liver. The disease had spread and was aggressive in its takeover.

With these new findings her medical team decided to stop chemotherapy. With the pain of the disease escalating, and the fact that Marnie required supervised care, a decision was made for Marnie to enter into a palliative care program. She was admitted to Victoria Hospital yesterday: September 28, 2015.

In our discussions with her doctors, end of life was expected anywhere from 2-4 weeks.

But this was not to be. In true Marnie fashion—we believe she had had enough: enough of hospitals, enough of the poking and prodding, and enough of fighting her courageous battle—she passed away less than 24 hours after admittance, at 1:00 a.m. September 29, 2015, with good friends and family at her side.

She went out on her own terms...to all who know her, this is not a surprise.

We received many notes of encouragement, hope, and prayer from all of you. We cannot begin to tell you how much that this has meant to us. We rode your positive energy and could have not have come this far without you...her team. We felt your love and know that you have been with us all the way on this difficult trek.

A true, heartfelt thank you to all who helped us out yesterday and late into the evening...you will never know how much that meant to our family.

God Bless...

For those participating in the run for the cure this weekend, we are still a go. There is no greater way to raise awareness and to honor how hard Marnie fought by taking part in this event.

We will provide more details as to our meeting place on Sunday in another email.

Much Love,

Marnie, Brian, Madison, and Brayden Foreman

"My heart has joined the Thousand, for my friend stopped running today."

— RICHARD ADAMS, WATERSHIP DOWN

BRIAN: *On the day that Marnie passed away, I was a complete mess: body shaking, uncontrollable sobbing, and an inability to speak.*

There'd been a series of tests, and we'd met with Dr. Ogaranko, who told us that the cancer had spread further, and that the treatment had stopped working. He explained there would be nothing more that they could do to help Marnie.

We discussed palliative care, and end of life. The doctor thought perhaps two to four weeks might be managed.

That's the part when I fell apart. But, when I looked over at Marnie, I had never seen her more calm or at peace. She gripped my hand and told me it was okay. She was okay. She had fought and incredible battle. She had had enough, and she knew it was over. We held hands for what seemed like hours; we both fell asleep from exhaustion.

I left the hospital about 2:30 in the afternoon to pick up Brayden from school and take him to hockey tryouts. I'd arranged for three of her close friends Jane, Tracey, and Sherri, to come sit with her at the hospital until I brought the kids back later that evening. Madison was working late and was in her room when Brayden and I came home from the rink. My plan was to meet both of the kids to tell them the news that the doctors were stopping treatment and admitting mom into palliative care.

When I got home, Madison was in tears. She said, "I know something is wrong, Dad."

And thus began the toughest conversation of my life.

We spoke about our ability to make mom's stay in palliative care as comfortable as possible. We would bring in her favorite board games to play, take in photo albums to share our memories, made sure to pack her comfortable pajamas so she'd feel at home, and we agreed we'd cuddle and hold her as much as possible.

We had a plan, and were ready to set it in action.

When we got to the hospital, we were greeted by Tracey (a close friend, and a nurse by profession) who told us that things had progressed drastically since I'd left earlier that afternoon.

Marnie was not going to die in two-to-four weeks. Marnie was dying now.

They had been trying to reach me but I had not answered (I'd turned off my phone so as not to interrupt my conversation with the kids).

Just like other parts of our cancer journey, we were thrown for another loop.

As Madison, Brayden, and I entered the room we saw Marnie surrounded by her Mom and Dad, and close friends.

She did not have the ability to speak.

When we approached her bed and began to speak to her she opened her eyes. She had the ability to listen.

The kids were able to tell her they loved her. They hugged and kissed her and said their goodbyes.

This was the last time she opened her eyes.

I sat with Marnie for the rest of the night; right up until she took her last breath.

Meanwhile, one of Marnie's close friends, Tammie, was on her way back from vacation, and landed at the Winnipeg airport in time to get to the hospital in time to say goodbye. I believe that Marnie held on to honor their bond.

Shortly after Tammie's arrival, Marnie passed away.

We never got to have a final conversation. I never got to say a final goodbye.

As I held her hand, I told her how much I loved her, and how proud of her I was for the epic battle she'd fought. I told her that she'd done a wonderful job in raising our children and instilling the values that they possess and will carry for the rest of their lives. I thanked her for all of the amazing times we had together and for making me a better person. I thanked her for being her. She was truly one in a million.

We learned it was okay to cry.

It (Mom's cancer) really did bring our family closer together, and I learned never to take anything for granted because this can really happen to anyone.

~Madison

At first, when I was eleven, and Mom and Dad told Madison and me that Mom had been diagnosed with breast cancer, I couldn't believe it. Of course, as a young kid, I thought of what the worst possibilities could've been, which eventually turned into reality by losing her.

~ Brayden

PLAYER PROFILE ~ JERSEY RETIRED

(taken directly and chronologically from the eulogy and shared over the chapters of this book)

"*I have thanked many people today, but I have one more person that I have to recognize.*

I need to thank Marnie; she used to joke with me that I was the educated one in the family, but she could not have been more wrong. She taught me so many things.

She taught me that there was a life outside the perimeter highway.

She insisted that we could never go to bed angry and, believe me, we had many a late night.

She taught me to be a parent with the empathy, support, and patience required.

She showed me selflessness and sacrifice as she allowed me to chase my career dreams.

There were many weeks where she was alone with the kids while I was traveling across Canada fulfilling my job aspirations.

She showed me what courage and determination look like.

The last three years she fought like no one I have ever seen. She had an incredibly strong will and did not want to let anyone down.

She taught me what real beauty is.

When you go through this journey your physical appearance goes through many changes. This was something that really bothered her. (But) it did not matter to me. Her heart shone through and she became more beautiful to me every day. I did not miss an opportunity to take off her now famous, black baseball cap and give her a peck on her head.

She gave me the opportunity to love deeper than I ever thought was possible.

Lastly I want to thank you for our two beautiful children whose values rise from your love and care. I will do my best to carry on your tradition. I will be there for them always and will continue to remind them of the love and pride their mother had for them in her heart.

I love you Marn. You fought an epic battle, and it is now time to rest in peace."

ADDENDUM

**This is the part no one wants to talk about,
but is essential for us to share, and, of
course, optional for each reader.**

—BRIAN FOREMAN

When the world as you've known it stops, and though you've thought a lot about what it will be like when your loved one is gone, it's surreal to see that the world actually does not stop. It doesn't even slow down. It's like the carousel keeps going around, and you're not sure when or how to jump onto the spinning platform, let alone get up on a horse.

Sure I had been thinking about what life would be like when she was gone, but all of a sudden, she was.

Nothing really prepares you for the thought of planning a funeral. May you find some guidance in my account of how Marnie's was planned.

It's funny how many things turn back to our community and our hockey world. Through Brayden's hockey team we had a connection to a family that own and run a funeral home. Therefore, we were fortunate to have John and Karen Leggat and the staff at Cropo Funeral Home guide us through the process. And it is a process.

The first thing on my mind was, how will I write an obituary?

Many templates exist on the internet. It's a way to see the structure. Pick up a newspaper and there are lots of examples of how others have honored their loved ones. But ultimately it's a bittersweet task.

I found a picture that captured her spirit. And I involved family in writing a tribute.

There is no right or wrong way to compose an obituary. Just your way.

Cremation or burial? I suggest you have this conversation before you are diagnosed with an illness. Something you think about and take care of earlier in life; and put it in your will.

In our case we chose cremation. There was no way in the world we were going to have any bit of cancer left in Marnie's body. We wanted it gone from her forever.

What type of casket? What style of urn? How much should you spend? Would your loved one have liked it?

The questions and choices are overwhelming. Simplify the process, be gentle with yourself.

We ended up going with a very elegant pewter urn, and decorated it with a breast cancer ribbon necklace to honor Marnie's courageous fight.

What type of flowers? Again, be easy on yourself. Don't get mired in catalogues of information.

Flowers were easy for us. Marnie loved daisies, and this is what she was going to have beside her.

One of the most difficult decisions can be where to hold the funeral. How many people will come? Will the venue hold everyone?

We went through a list of locations before we settled on the Calvary Temple in downtown Winnipeg. Our struggle was with the size of the funeral. We were active in our community and had developed relationships with many people. We were happy with the recommendation from John and Karen as almost 1000 people came to honor Marnie.

Who would perform the funeral service? We did not belong to a church, and did not want to have a person we did not know oversee the proceedings. Marnie and I had renewed our wedding vows on our tenth anniversary. A lifelong friend, Reverend Glenn, had helped us then. It seemed appropriate to invite Glenn back for the funeral. He knew us. We knew he'd make it a heartfelt experience for all.

Who will speak at the funeral? Will there be prayers? We wanted a true celebration of life, and with this in mind we chose lifelong friends and family members to deliver relevant prayers and to tell stories about Marnie and their experiences together. This brought out her true character and allowed everyone in attendance to know Marnie better.

One of the toughest decisions for me was delivering the Eulogy. This was something that I wanted to do. It was my chance to say goodbye and to have closure with Marnie.

It was also my way to remember all the good that we had, the family we had created, and the memories that we made. It was an incredibly hard thing to do, to maintain composure and speak about my wife.

I drew from her strength, told her story, and I am so thankful that I was able to do this.

*O*ther considerations?

With Marnie's love for Country Music it seemed appropriate to have someone perform some songs.

One of our favorite things to do was to go for drinks and appetizers at a nearby restaurant on warm summer evenings. It was there we'd enjoyed musician Garret Neiles, the perfect choice for her service.

The kids, family, and I went through old photo albums and created poster boards of Marnie's life allowed us to reminisce.

Madison created a wonderful PowerPoint presentation about her mom's life. It streamed through the church prior to the service, and after in the reception hall. A special tribute through the eyes of a mother's daughter.

*A*nd how to cater for so many people?

Enter, again, our friends the Sartor family, and Calabria Market. They stepped in and provided nourishment for us and our funeral attendees.

It's not an easy process. And it culminates in an even more difficult day. With the love and support of friends and family, we moved through it consciously. We were determined not to go through the motions and have 'no memory' of the celebration. It is painful to open oneself to all of the things that have to be done, but it is also incredibly therapeutic to experience each part of the plan in honouring your loved one. It is also important to know yourself well enough to step back and allow others to help.

Epilogue

PLAY BY PLAY

Dear Team Marnie,

We're beyond the one year mark of Marnie's passing. Not a day goes by that we don't think of her. Although it has been hard we draw our strength from her journey and apply it to our everyday lives. The 'firsts' were definitely the most challenging. Her Birthday, Christmas, New Year, and Mother's Day were events that played with our emotions, and made us appreciate her even more.

We were sad that she wasn't there when Brayden won both the city and provincial hockey championships. Likewise, not seeing Madison flourish in in her first year of University. And, neither was she able to bake for her husband's 50th and partake in the birthday celebrations. We say she did not witness these events, but her presence was certainly felt

Brian, Madison, and Brayden

TIME OUT

"I think we dream so we don't have to be apart for so long. If we're in each other's dreams, we can be together all the time."

WINNIE THE POOH—A.A. MILNE

RECAP

Our lives have returned to as normal as they can be—organizing our next family get-away, registering for school and sports, and visiting with friends and family. On that note, we've a new member, a Goldendoodle ball of energy, Bear. And we wrote this book, putting the final stamp on it when it felt time to do so.

COACH'S CORNER

What we did to help ourselves.

We have relied heavily on each other and immersed ourselves in our own activities.

> *BRIAN: I took some time off work to gather my thoughts and learn how to run a household. I had to learn the routines of school, the drop-offs, the pick-ups, homework, and parent teacher interviews.*
>
> *Madison helped immensely in teaching me what 'mom' did.*
>
> *I increased my daily exercise and took great solace in bike rides through the park, or long runs. I started reading again; not research reading, but delving back into the word of Michael Connelly, John Grisham, and Mitch Albom—a refreshing change.*
>
> *Most evenings, I'm the cook. Unfamiliar with the aisles at Sobeys, Safeway and Wal-Mart, I had a steep learning curve.*
>
> *I had to learn how to make lunch…*

Madison: I kept up my studies at the University of Winnipeg, attending part time until Christmas. After that I upped my courses to that of a full time student. I'm currently student teaching. Dad and I spend many evenings talking about school, my friends, and, generally, about my day. It's true, school is a distraction for me. I think each of us have thrown ourselves into our activities because we know Mom would have expected nothing less than full participation, and because it helps us honour her without having to 'think too deeply' about what we've been through.

Brayden: For me, I'm pretty quiet. Dad says this is normal for a teenager. It doesn't mean I don't think about stuff, and it doesn't mean I just echo what my sister and dad say. I've been really lucky to be surrounded by teammates and friends. Being in sports has lot of advantages. I love hockey and it's something I can put my brain and my body into—it's physical and mental. Playing sports and going to school makes for a super busy life. Of course there's still room for Mom, but I say what I have to say and I don't repeat it a gazillion times. I know it's okay to be me, and I have lots of support from Dad, and from the family.

What others did that was helpful.

They continued to check in on us. Texts, e-mails, cards, phone calls, invites to events, let us know that they were still there. All of this has helped us in adjusting to our new life. An invitation to a Jets game, an offer of help to run an errand, or just heading out for a beer with friends have been appreciated.

School counsellors earned their pay as they helped communicate our situation to the many teachers and professors that our children dealt with.

Hockey coaches and hockey families demonstrated empathy beyond belief. They helped at the funeral, they provided meals, wide shoulders and patient listening skills demonstrated they understood what we were going through.

At work, bosses, colleagues, and staff provided much needed space and time. Workloads were shared. Co-workers demonstrated exemplary tolerance for forgetfulness, and the occasional 'out of character' mood change.

Folks helped us expedite needed tests, gave us advice, and provided comfort in any way they could. We know these individuals would not want recognition but, Morley and Char, we don't know where we would have been without you.

What the professionals did.

They were there with us right to the end. With heavy hearts they had expressed our need for palliative care and helped us with end of life expectations, and afterwards, they shed tears with us.

They called after Marnie's passing to express their condolences. They wrote e-mails expressing their feelings. They attended her funeral service.

They went above and beyond and, once again, proved that they cared. Marnie had as big of an impact on their lives as they did on ours. They became like family and were an incredible team.

THREE STARS

- Parents: understand the strength and resilience of your kids. Make sure that you create an avenue for them to talk and express their feelings. 'If you build it, they will come...'
- Medical teams: cordial at first, relationships develop into trusted bonds between family and health care providers. It may be a partnership you hope you don't have to make (you might remember what Marnie said to one doctor: "It's not nice to meet you."), but when circumstances dictate medical intervention, invest in connection; you'll be grateful you did.
- Friends and community: friends look after each other; mind and soul. Countless acts of kindness and selflessness that can never be re-paid. No matter your role in a cancer journey, be it your own or that of a loved one or an acquaintance: accept it from others and/or pay it forward.

OVERTIME

BRIAN: Three months after Marnie's death I consulted my company's Employee Assistance Program. My biggest issue was my inability to fall asleep or stay sleeping. I also wanted to ensure that I was on the right track to emotional healing.

It was well worth the time as they gave me some great resources on relaxation and meditation. It also gave me confidence that I was on the right path for myself, and for Madison and Brayden. I continue to be strong enough to ask for help when I need it.

http://www.just-a-minute.org/ - Go to the Resource Centre

http://www.learnmeditationonline.org/elearning/course/index?lang=en

LEGACY OF A PLAYER

Throughout our cancer journey—before and after Marnie's passing—we met many phenomenal people. We drew inspiration from the people fighting the same fight we were. In discussion, with Marnie, we'd talked about a way to celebrate the milestone 50th birthday which would arrive in 2016. (Brian's).

We decided to fundraise for the 'cause'. First, there needs to be a cure. Second, not everyone had the perks we had in having a multitude of family and friends, connections to facilities in the city, and a measure of financial security.

BRIAN: Prior to Father's Day 2016, I began training, and on Father's Day 2016, I joined a team of supporters to run the full Manitoba Marathon to raise awareness and funds for CancerCare Manitoba Foundation to support and alleviate the burden put on cancer patients and their families. A chance to make their lives a little easier.

The 'Miles for Marnie' initiative gave us the opportunity to positively contribute to the efforts, battles, and journeys of the many cancer families we've met. There were so many: ones that offered advice, made us smile, and gave us hope. It also allows us to pay it forward to all those who will require support in the future.

We are happy to report that at the time of writing this epilogue, over $350,000 has been raised in Marnie's name. A fantastic legacy for phenomenal woman.

It is our sincere hope that the cure of cancer is soon discovered.

We know that until then, some of you will beat this disease and live long and happy lives. For you and your loved ones, we could not be happier.

We also know that, for others, as was our reality, life will be much shorter than anticipated. Please know that wherever you are, we grieve with you, and we include the memory of your loved ones in our continued fundraising and quest for a support and cure. After all, we are a team.

September 29, 2016

Dear Marnie,

I truly cannot believe that a year has gone by since your passing.

It has been tough as we experienced the many "firsts" without you; Birthdays, Anniversaries, the Holidays, and vacations were met with mixed emotions as we honored your memory while missing your presence.

We have our good days, and still experience the challenges of missing your ever-present laugh and smile, your positive outlook on life, your ear to listen to, and the love and lore you passed on to our family and friends.

Your kids are amazing. The values you instilled in them are shining through. A strong commitment to school, while persevering through sport, keeps them very busy. They do this without complaint and are successful in their educational outputs. There is no doubt that they are your creation and benefited from the time you had with them.

Marnie, your constant preaching of respect has paid off. The integrity entrenched in both kids is ever present in their daily lives. Respect for their schools, their teachers and professors as well as their classmates and teammates is demonstrated daily. You would be so proud. A lady and a gentleman for sure......

I have been missing you a lot lately. Our late night conversations, our reality checks of what is happening around us, but more importantly—just you. The time we spent together. The time I took for granted, but wish I had so much of it back.

I hope you are surrounded by great ones you love: your Dad, your Auntie Lauree, your Uncle Cam, Grandpa Russ, and Grandma Heather. That would make one great curling team!

You will always be with me in my heart. I search for you in the stars when I am flying, or on a dark lit lake with a twinkling sky. At those times I feel closer to you, and in that I find peace.

You are missed so much. We are getting by on the life-lessons you taught us and instilled in our family

Grateful for the years we had together...

Love you,

Brian

WHEN TOMORROW STARTS WITHOUT ME

When tomorrow starts without me
And I'm not here to see
If the sun should rise and find your eyes
All filled with tears for me

I wish you wouldn't cry
The Way you did today
While thinking of the many things
We did not get to say

I know how much you love me
As much as I love you
Each time that you think of me
I know you will miss me too

When tomorrow starts with out me
Please try to understand
That an angel came and called my name
And took me by the hand

The angel said my place was ready
In heaven far above
And That I would have to leave behind
All those I Dearly Love

But When I walked through Heaven's Gates
I felt so much at home
When GOD looked down and smiled at me
From his golden throne

He said This Is Eternity
And All I promised you
Today for life on earth is done
But Here it starts a new

I promise no tomorrow
For today will always last
And Since each day's the exact same way
There is no longing for the past

So When Tomorrow starts without me
Do not think we're apart
For every time you think of me
Remember I'm right here in your heart
Author: David M Romano

Made in the USA
Charleston, SC
05 February 2017